VAT Explained

VAT Explained

The business man's and manager's guide to value added tax

John Chown
Taxation Correspondent, Financial Times

 KOGAN PAGE (Associates)

First published 1972

Published by Kogan Page (Associates) Limited,
16 Gray's Inn Road, London WC1X 8BR

© 1972 John Chown

Typesetting by Dahling Dahling, 331 Gray's Inn Road,
London WC14 8PX

Printed by Compton Printing Limited,
London and Aylesbury

SBN 85038 022 7

Contents

Acknowledgements

I would like to thank those who helped with the writing of this book. In particular Mr. John Reynolds and Mrs. Zara Lupton read through the manuscript and made a number of helpful comments. Mr. D. A. van Waardenburg read through the sections dealing with European experience: his mastery of his subject was such that he returned copy thoroughly annotated, almost by return of post.

Miss Hilary Smith, Mrs. Brenda Moss and Mrs. Jean Hobson typed the various drafts of the manuscripts efficiently and speedily at a time when our office was not without other distractions.

My wife Vera not only put up with a complete breakdown of our social life for three weekends: but also undertook last year the study of European VAT systems on which this book is partly based.

J.F.C.
April 1972.

1. The General Principles of VAT

As from 1st April, 1973 purchase tax and selective employment tax (SET) are to be abolished and replaced by a Value Added Tax (VAT). The necessary legislation has been tabled as part of the 1972 Finance Bill. This is subject to amendment as it goes through its parliamentary stages, and in any case the Bill when it becomes an Act will have to be supplemented by Customs and Excise Regulations setting out in more detail the treatment of particular situations.

VAT is in concept a simple tax. It has already been introduced in eight other European countries. It will directly involve some 1½ million traders, far more than the 60,000 who were involved with purchase tax. Most, if not all, of these will at present be concerned with income tax (or corporation tax) and probably with SET.

VAT will be chargeable at a single standard rate (probably 10% to begin with) on the supply of all goods and services within the UK, and on imports, subject to certain exceptions. The characteristic feature of VAT is that it applies on *all* transactions, including those between traders. Where a trader buys a product or pays for a service with a VAT content he will be able to deduct this "input tax" from the amount he owes to the Customs and Excise in respect of VAT on his own sales, the "output tax". This means that the tax paid by each trader will normally be 10% of his own "value added" that is to say his sales less his *taxed* purchases. There is however no need actually to calculate this value added. The amount due to the Customs and Excise is quite simply found by taking 10% of all taxable sales in the period and deducting the total VAT element on all purchases invoiced to the trader during the same period. This is simple enough calculation in principle, but it will be necessary to adapt book-keeping systems to throw up the VAT content in both purchase and sales invoices. Examples given below should make the position clear.

Some types of transactions and some categories of trader will be exempt from VAT. This is not quite so favourable as it may sound, as explained in Chapter 3. Other transactions are in principle subject to the tax, but at a rate of zero. This "zero rating" produces a much more favourable result, again as explained in Chapter 3. It is perfectly possible to apply VAT at multiple rates and indeed five out of the eight countries already imposing VAT do so at multiple rates. The UK has opted for the simpler single rate system.

Exports are zero rated. The export customer pays no tax and the actual exporter can obtain a reclaim of the taxes paid at previous stages. VAT is *not* an export subsidy: foreign customers do not at present pay purchase tax. The change might very slightly improve export competitiveness for reasons explained later. Imports are subject to VAT at the time of entry. This is in addition to any customs duties which might also be payable.

VAT is not a tax on traders. It is passed forward to the ultimate customers and is a tax on *consumption* in the United Kingdom. Despite the zero rating of foods, books, newspapers and certain other categories it will be a much broader based tax than purchase tax. In particular it will catch services which previously escaped purchase tax and were only caught in a rather haphazard way by the clumsy SET. Because it is a broader based tax it can be at a generally moderate rate and will remove many previous distortions. For instance, some goods which last year were subject to purchase tax of 45% will become much cheaper, while others which escaped the tax altogether will be rather more expensive. It will thus (more or less) bring to an end the idea that the Government should discourage certain types of expenditure by taxing them more heavily. There will still be heavy excise taxes on tobacco, alcohol and petrol and in principle there should be no change in the price of these highly taxed commodities. Cars will also have special treatment. In addition to VAT at 10%, there will be a special "car tax" at 10% on the *wholesale* value. Car tax will apply only to new, or newly imported cars. This compares with a 30% purchase tax, reduced for this year to 25%. There is the important distinction that purchase tax was levied on the wholesale while VAT will eventually be collected on the retail price.

If a car sells for £800 (excluding tax) at the wholesale level and the retailer wants a clear margin of £200 the tax free retail price would be £1000. With purchase tax at 25% on the wholesale price of £800, the all-in price is today £1200. With car tax £80 and VAT £108, the all-in price would be £1188.

The immediate economic effects of VAT are unlikely to be dramatic. There will be changes in relative prices but the rate structure chosen is unlikely to have much influence on the general level of prices in the UK.

The Chancellor announced that if he were fixing the rate of VAT today it would be 10%. He made it clear that the actual rate cannot be fixed until next year's budget. There is provision in the legislation for the initial rate to be anywhere within the range of between 7½% and 12½%, depending on the needs of economic management at the time. In addition, the Chancellor proposes to keep his "regulator" under VAT and indeed extend it from the former 10% either way to 20% in the course of a year. This might appear to create administrative complications but in practice, as I shall show in (Chapter 6) it does not.

Accounting for VAT is to be on a quarterly basis but to spread the administrative load the accounting periods will be staggered, so that about a third of all traders will have an accounting period ending at the end of each month. Payment will be due one month after the end of the accounting period. Certain traders will have an option to use a one month accounting period: this will be to the advantage of those who will have a net reclaim at the end of each period.

The first five chapters of this book give a general description of the principles of VAT. These are essential reading for all those concerned. Part 2 deals with special problems which will apply to most traders. It includes the transitional problems affecting a trader who already has purchase tax paid stocks at the start of the system. There are some categories of input for which a tax credit is denied, at present confined to private motor cars and some business entertainment. In certain circumstances the trader may become liable to VAT even without a formal sale. This would apply to goods for his own consumption and to self supply of taxable goods by an exempt trader. There are special problems concerned with hire purchase, leasing, purchasing of capital equipment and discounts and small traders. Also in this Part we discuss the likely effect of the tax on business liquidity.

Part 3 discusses the trades and transactions which are afforded special treatment. There is a full discussion on the categories granted exemption or zero rating in the UK. I explain briefly what happened in other European countries and also discuss some categories which receive special treatment in other countries but not here. Part 3 is organised in such a way that the reader can turn quickly to those sections which directly concern him. Part 4 deals with international transactions in exports and imports including services and intangibles such as patent and copyright licences. Part 5 discusses the economic arguments for and against VAT and also describes the history and experience of VAT in other countries. This Part can be omitted by those who want purely practical guidance, but those who can spare the time will find that an understanding of the background may help towards an understanding of the tax itself.

The Arithmetic of VAT

A "taxable person" is a trader who, as explained in Chapter 2, may be a company, a sole trader, a partnership or any other form of organisation. Assume that such a trader sells goods in a particular three month accounting period to the value of £100,000. He will have to add on to his invoices VAT of 10% amounting in all to £110,000. (Note that VAT is calculated on the price *exclusive* of the tax). In principle, therefore, there is £10,000 tax to be paid to the Customs and Excise. However, the trader may himself have bought goods costing £60,000 (tax exclusive) with 10% VAT amounting in all to £6,000 borne on these invoices. The amount actually payable to the Customs and Excise is therefore £4,000

(£10,000 output tax less £6,000 input tax). Ignoring tax the trader has sold goods for £100,000 based on purchases of £60,000. His "value added" is therefore £40,000. It does not matter whether this reflects wages, profits, purchase of exempt or zero rated goods, or a change in the level of stocks. There is no need to calculate the value added and no need to reconcile this with the quite different concepts of accounting profits or taxable profits.

In cash flow terms, including tax, the trader has paid £66,000 including VAT to his suppliers, and has received or will in due course receive £110,000 from his customers. This is a difference of £44,000 and after paying £4,000 to the Customs and Excise he is left once more with the £40,000 figure of value added. The trader is thus in exactly the same position, except possibly on the timing of cash flows, as if the tax did not exist. His customers have paid 10% more than they would have done in the absence of tax. If they are private individuals or exempt traders they would actually bear this tax as an extra cost of the goods. If they are themselves traders selling taxable (or zero rated) goods they will simply pass the tax through in exactly the same way.

From the trader's point of view, the position is simple, provided that all his sales are either of taxable or of zero rated goods and services. He adds 10% of all his sales to his invoices, except where the transaction is zero rated, and keeps an account of this, This is his "output tax". He also keeps an account of the VAT element in the purchase price of all goods and services invoiced to him, taking care to obtain a "tax invoice" in each case. This is his "input tax". At the end of each quarter he deducts the total input tax from the total output tax and pays the difference over, within a month, to the Customs and Excise. If the input tax exceeds the output tax, he claims a refund.

From the point of view of the customer, he will pay a 10% tax on the total retail price, but the tax will actually be collected only in part from the retailer. Customers who are not traders will normally think in "tax-inclusive" terms and will not have to concern themselves with the tax content.

The following illustration shows how the tax charge builds up as a product goes through its stages from the manufacturer to the consumer. It will be seen that the total tax is just 10% of the final selling price but the tax is collected at each different stage. It makes no difference to the total tax ultimately borne by the consumer, how many product stages are involved. The tax is borne on the final retail price unlike purchase tax which is borne on the wholesale price. In the example given a 10% VAT is equivalent to a 11.76% purchase tax imposed on a wholesale level. There is no necessary relationship between purchase tax rates and VAT rates as this will depend on the retail mark-up.

	£
Trader A makes components and sells to Trader B for (value added £ 4.00)	4.00
Trader B assembles and sells to Trader C (Wholesaler) for (value added £ 3.50)	7.50
Trader C sells to Trader D (retailer) for (value added £ 1.00)	8.50
Trader D sells to customer for (value added £ 1.50)	10.00

All the above figures are net of VAT.

		£
Trader A pays VAT of		0.40
Trader B accounts for VAT output tax of	0.75	
but deducts input tax of	0.40	
paying a net sum of		0.35
Trader C accounts for VAT output tax of	0.85	
but deducts input tax of	0.75	
paying a net sum of		0.10
Trader D accounts for VAT output tax of	1.00	
but deducts input tax of	0.85	
paying a net sum of		0.15
TOTAL VAT borne by customers		1.00

Trader B (for instance) would be invoiced by Trader A as follows:-

Goods purchased	4.00
plus VAT	0.40
total payable	4.40

Trader B would then invoice Trader C as follows:-

Goods Purchased	7.50
plus VAT	0.75
total payable	8.25

He would receive £8.25 and pay out £4.40 leaving him with the difference of £3.85. He would then have a liability to pay £0.35 VAT, and once he had settled that he would be left with this gross margin of £3.50 — exactly the same as if VAT did not exist.

The various traders involved do not have to make individual calculations of this kind. As explained above, all they have to do each quarter is add the total output VAT on their sale and deduct the input VAT actually charged on goods sold to them during the same period.

Alternative VAT Systems

VAT could equally well be levied on the price inclusive of tax. France did originally and Sweden still does. The following example shows that the effective rate is different in each case.

	VAT at 10% on	
	VAT inclusive price	VAT exclusive price
(1) Price before VAT	90	100
(2) VAT	10	10
(3) Price including VAT	100	110
VAT as % of (1)	11.11	10
VAT as % of (3)	10	9.09

15

A retailer who sells only for cash to consumers who do not require a tax invoice should remember that VAT is not one tenth, but one *eleventh* (9.09%) of the total cash price. This is because the 10% VAT is levied only on the exclusive price, which is ten elevenths of the total cash price.

From a practical point of view what the trader needs is to devise a form of accounting which will show at the three month period the total VAT content in both purchases and sales. This will be subject to audit by the Customs and Excise. There is no requirement that records and accounts have to be kept in any particular prescribed form. Existing accounting methods can be adapted in whatever form seems to be most convenient to the trader and his adviser. The minimum requirement will probably mean an extra column in the purchase and sales journals.

VAT and Stock Levels

VAT is a tax on the supply of goods and services and not a tax on money flows. The time of supply can be either the date of dispatch or the date of invoice. In strict law this is whichever is earlier. In most cases the Customs will probably accept an invoice basis. The calculation will then have to be made on *invoices* issued and *invoices* received during the accounting period. Time of payment will not be relevant.

It also does not matter whether the transactions result in an increase in stock during the period. For instance in one quarterly accounting period a particular trader's purchases may exceed his sales even though he is trading profitably and has in the long run a positive "value added". His purchases might be £120,000 to which £12,000 VAT is added making a total cost of £132,000. If his sales are only £100,000 on which there is a VAT content of £10,000, he will be able to get a reclaim at the end of the quarter of £2,000 from the Customs and Excise. Normally no questions will be asked as to why this happened and it will only be necessary to satisfy the authorities that it did happen. There could of course be a number of explanations. Trade may be seasonal. A toy importer and wholesaler will have an excess of deliveries in the quarter to 31st October selling these on to retailers in the quarter covering Christmas. In this case there might be a very high payment to the Customs and Excise in the following quarter.

In other cases stock fluctuations may simply be a random effect of the timing of transactions. This would be particularly true of a business whose turnover reflected a small number of large transactions. Changes in stock levels might also reflect a policy decision to anticipate expected price changes. Note particularly that one might get the same temporary recovery effect where purchases were high in a particular quarter because they included capital equipment. As discussed in more detail in Chapter 10 there is in fact to be no special treatment of such cases and no restrictions on immediate refund.

In principle, therefore, VAT is quite simple and straightforward. The elementary principle should now be clear and we can turn to some of the complications and special cases.

2. The Concept of the "Taxable Person"

A "taxable person" is defined in Clause 4 of the Bill as "a person who makes or intends to make taxable supplies". In practice, this means any trader carrying on business within the United Kingdom unless his business is entirely in goods and services exempt on one of the categories discussed in Chapter 13. There is also an exemption for traders with a turnover of less than £5,000 per annum: this is discussed in more detail below. A "taxable person" can be an individual trader or professional man, a company, a partnership, a local authority, a public corporation, a cooperative society or any other form of organisation capable of carrying on business.

Taxable persons must register with the Commissioners of Customs and Excise. Full publicity will be given to the procedure starting in October 1972 and registration will be compulsory for everyone who has, or expects to have, a turnover in taxable goods exceeding £5,000 per annum. Registered traders will be allotted a serial number and will be told which cycle of months will apply to them. Some traders will be allotted as accounting periods the quarters ending 31st March, 30th June, 30th September and 31st December. Others will make up their accounts to 30th April or to 31st May and the corresponding quarters in each case. Traders will be able to choose a one month instead of a quarterly accounting period if they are likely to have net reclaims.

Groups of Companies
The concept of "taxable person" is a very flexible one. Clause 21 provides that groups of companies under common control may elect to be treated as a single taxable person. One of the companies is selected as the "representative

member" of the group and becomes liable to account for VAT on behalf of the group as a whole. Transactions between members of the group are ignored for the purposes of VAT. The amount of tax payable at the end of each accounting period is the total output on the sales by all the group companies to non-members of the group less the total input tax invoiced on purchases to all members of the group from outside. This could considerably simplify administration.

The definition of a group for this purpose is more flexible than any of the definitions for corporation tax purposes. Companies can be treated as members of a group provided that they are all resident within the United Kingdom, and one of them controls each of the others; one person (whether a body corporate or an individual) controls all of them; or two or more individuals carrying on business in partnership control all of them. The definition of "control" is the usual Companies Act definition but extended in the case of an individual or any individuals to apply as if they were companies for this purpose. There does not appear to be any *obligation* to opt for group treatment and it also seems that one or more companies within a group could be left out of the option. For instance, a group might have an export subsidiary which, if treated as a separate entity would normally be in a position to make a substantial reclaim from the Customs and Excise. If its purchases from other group companies were £100,000 per month and these were entirely sold abroad the reclaim would be £10,000 per month. The group as a whole including the export company might typically have to pay over VAT of £15,000 per month or £45,000 per quarter. Group treatment does not affect the total VAT payable (except possibly in the case of partially exempt traders — see Chapter 9) but it may affect the timing of the payment. If it were possible to elect to exclude the export company from the group and for it to opt for a one month accounting period, the net effect would be to bring forward the reclaim of £10,000 per month by an average period of six weeks (half of three months) while giving the rest of the group the normal length of credit. This procedure may well be ruled out by Regulations yet to be issued but if it were possible, the effect of partial election would be to give the group an interest free loan from the Government averaging £15,000.

Partnerships

Partnerships are treated as taxable persons in the firm name and no account shall be taken for VAT purposes of changes in the composition of the partnership. This, again, differs from the income tax treatment but is sensible and straightforward. (Clause 22). Regulations are to be published in due course on the application of VAT to member's clubs. (Clause 23 [2]).

Divisions of Companies

A company may elect to have different divisions registered as separate "taxable persons". (Clause 23 [1]). This is a sensible and simplifying provision which will be particularly important where a company carries on both exempt and non-exempt transactions. It was originally thought that it might be necessary for such companies to divide their activities into separate subsidiaries to ensure the most favourable allocation of input. Subject to Regulations, and the attitude of the Customs and Excise, it might again be possible to hive off as a separate division any part of the business which was likely to make net reclaims with the favourable effect on cash flow. This provision and that dealing with groups do mean that a company or group of companies can organise itself into as many or as few taxable persons as may be convenient for administration or accountability for VAT purposes without disturbing the underlying corporate structure. A single company can be several "taxable persons" while a group of many companies can be one, or two or more.

Non-residents

Non-residents can be taxable persons. Clause 24 provides that the Commissioners of Customs and Excise may by notice in writing nominate an agent to be accountable for the non-resident. Where a non-resident buys goods for re-sale within the United Kingdom it may be in his interests to become a taxable person. A non-resident company or individual who trades in the UK through a branch "permanent establishment" or "dependent agent" will be liable to income tax or to corporation tax on the profits derived from "trading within" the United Kingdom. Many non-resident businesses have taken pains to avoid this status. Because of the risk of the "sandwich effect" (see Chapter 3) some foreign companies or businesses will now actually *want* to be "taxable persons" for VAT purposes. Whether it will be possible to achieve this status without being deemed to be "trading within" the United Kingdom for income tax or corporation tax purposes is a still open and very interesting question. There are also unresolved questions on international trade in services where there is a permanent establishment both within and outside the UK — see Chapter 22.

Small Traders

Traders with a turnover of £5,000 or less per annum are exempt from registration. They can nevertheless register if they think that it would be to their advantage to do so. This raises two questions for the small trader — *need* I register? If not, *should* I register?

The "£5,000" rule is in fact spelt out in a little more detail. If turnover exceeds £1,750 in one quarter *or* a total of £3,000 in two successive quarters, *or* a total of £4,250 in three successive quarters or £5,000 in four quarters (whether or not they constitute a calendar year) the trader will become liable to registration. He may avoid registration if he can satisfy the Commissioners that in spite of these figures his total taxable supplies for the forthcoming year will not exceed £5,000. A registered trader can cease to be registered (subject to his right to elect to continue) if his turnover has been below £4,000 for each of two years or if the Commissioners are satisfied that his taxable supplies in the year about to begin would be £4,000 or less.

It is, of course, a very small business that sells only £5,000 per annum of goods or services. Exemption will typically cover rather larger businesses dealing mainly in exempt goods and services and only incidentally in taxable goods and services, or the part-timer. It may also include services rendered by a jobbing handyman, plumber, gardener or the like where there are few expenses and the turnover represents almost entirely personal income. If such people are mainly serving private householders rather than businesses it may suit them somewhat to alter their business methods to claim exemption.

Take the case of a plumber working entirely on household repairs. In the course of a year he buys on behalf of his customers supplies worth £6,000 at normal retail prices but obtains a discount of £1,000. His gross charges are £10,000. He has expenses (advertising, telephone and motor cycle maintenance and fuel) of £500 leaving him with a profit of £4,500. With VAT he would have to charge his customers £11,000: at this level of turnover he would not be eligible for exemption. He might consider no longer buying and reselling materials and simply charge for his labour. On this basis he would arrange for the builders merchant to invoice the customers direct for the £6,000 of purchases adding on VAT of £600. (The plumber could still collect the materials on behalf of the customer). Instead of receiving a discount from the builders merchant he might be paid an introductory commission of an equivalent amount. He would invoice customers only for work done and his turnover including commission would be just under the £5,000. He would have saved his customers £400 while maintaining his income, or if his competitors were charging VAT, he might be able to increase his own profit margin by that figure. Better still, he could arrange with the builders merchant to pass the discount on to his customers, and make a corresponding increase in his own charge. This would save another £100.

The exemption limits in most European countries is typically much smaller. In Denmark it is as little as £360 per annum. Several countries have a special system for relatively small retailers which gives an approximate answer without administrative complications. For instance, in Belgium, retailers with purchases of up to about £12,000 are excluded from the VAT system. However, wholesalers and others supplying such retailers add on to the invoice not only the normal VAT but also the supplementary tax designed to approximate the tax that would have been collected from the retailer on his own margin.

Should a small trader register even if he is eligible for exemption? He should consider it if a material proportion of his input has borne VAT and if the bulk of his customers are traders in a position to recover the input tax. For instance, a small trader had a turnover of £4,000 before the introduction of VAT. He buys goods at a cost of £2,000 plus £200 VAT. To preserve his margins as an exempt trader he would have to raise his prices so that his total sales were £4,200. If he becomes a taxable trader he could preserve the position by keeping his own invoice price at £4,000 adding £400 VAT, recovering the £200 input tax and paying the other £200 to the Customs and Excise. From this point of view both procedures have exactly the same result.

From the point of view of the customers, the position is not the same. If his customers were private individuals they would have to pay more in the second case: if he remained exempt while his competitors were larger non-exempt traders he would have a price advantage. If he increased his prices exactly in line with those of his competitors he could sell his goods for £4,400 increasing his profits by £200.

On the other hand, if his customers were other traders the situation would be reversed. They would rather buy from his competitors at £44 a unit including £4 of creditable VAT than from him at £42 per unit with no creditable VAT. In this case he would be better advised to register. Indeed, on the example given if more than half his customers are traders he should register on the simple arithmetic of the situation. He may still choose not to register to avoid administrative complications.

The Regulations will certainly provide that a trader cannot split himself up into a number of "taxable persons" in such a way that some or all of the parts can claim exemption on the grounds that turnover is below £5,000. Similarly, there will almost certainly be a provision to *require* group treatment where companies under common control of other companies seek to claim the under £5,000 exemption. It is unlikely that any scope will be allowed for this kind of fiddle. On the other hand the attitude may be a little more permissive where a particular subsidiary mainly supplies exempt goods and services and only supplies taxable goods to the value of less than £5,000 as a small incidental part of its activity.

3. The Difference Between Zero Rating and Exemption

Although the United Kingdom is to impose VAT at a single rate, certain categories of goods and services will be either "exempted" or "zero rated". The actual categories involved are discussed in Chapters 12 to 14. The distinction between exemption and zero rating is vitally important to the understanding of VAT.

First of all, exemption. This is not as attractive a status as it may at first sound. An exempt trader is outside the VAT system and provided that all his activities are exempt he is at least spared any administrative involvement with VAT. The difficulty is that the exempt trader cannot recover the VAT borne on his own inputs. The following example should illustrate.

	Pre VAT	Post VAT
Purchases by exempt trader	4,000	4,000
on which VAT	—	400
	4,000	4,400
Exempt trader's own "value added"	6,000	6,000
Sales to customers	10,000	10,400

It will be seen that the exempt trader's customers are, in effect, bearing £400 VAT in the cost of the goods he sells. This compares with £1,000 that would have been borne were the goods subject to VAT at the normal rate. If the customers are ultimate consumers or other exempt traders, this is an improvement. It is nevertheless not as good as zero rating.

Where sales are zero rated it means that the trader *is* liable to VAT but at a rate of zero. The trader calculates his output tax at zero, but is still allowed as a credit his input tax which means that he can make a reclaim of all the tax paid at previous stages on his inputs. Look at the same example on the assumption that the trader is zero rated rather than exempted. It will be seen that the ultimate customers now pay only £10,000. There is no VAT content either direct or indirect in the cost.

Purchases	4,000
on which VAT	400
	4,400
Sales (zero rated)	10,000
on which VAT	NIL
Price to customer	10,000

Trader *recovers* £400 VAT input tax from the Customs and Excise.

Apart from food and certain other categories the most important application of zero rating is to exports. This is discussed in more detail in Chapter 20. It means that the export customer genuinely escapes the VAT levies not only at the final, but at all intermediate stages.

Where sales are made to an ultimate domestic consumer, exemption can be regarded as a second best to zero rating. The price to the customer includes an indirect element of VAT but there is no tax on the value added at the last stage or on exempt transactions at earlier stages. However, where the customer is a taxable trader, exemption may actually give a worse answer than a full VAT liability. This is because of what is known as the "sandwich effect".

Going back to the original example, assume that a customer of the exempt trader is a taxable trader. He has to pay £104 which includes an element of £4 of indirect VAT. Because this is not directly shown on the invoice he cannot claim this as a creditable input tax and must add on a full VAT charge at the next stage. His customer will bear in total tax of more than 10%. From the point of view of the taxable trader he would much rather the supplier was also taxable.

The supplier would then charge £110 and although this is a larger sum £10 of VAT would be creditable.

Exemption therefore is not nearly as desirable as it sounds, especially where there are considerable taxable inputs and especially where a significant proportion of customers are themselves taxable traders. The private customer who buys exempt goods or services is still bearing an element of indirect VAT that was charged on the suppliers' own purchases. For him the situation is somewhere between zero rating and full tax liability. Where a taxable trader buys from an exempt trader the total VAT charge is actually increased.

4. Procedure

The Customs and Excise will be issuing detailed instructions to traders in due course. These instructions will probably be clear and precise and will explain exactly what traders will have to do. In the meantime, I am attempting in this chapter to describe what will probably happen so that those concerned can at least start making their plans.

Taxable Person Or Not?

A trader must register as a taxable person unless all his transactions are in exempt goods or services (see Chapter 13) or unless his taxable outputs are likely to be £5,000 or less per annum (see Chapter 2). If he does supply taxable goods or services and his sales are below this figure he can register if he so wishes and it may be to his advantage to do so.

A trader, all of whose sales are zero rated, will nevertheless have to register. Apart from the legal requirement, it will be materially to his advantage so to do.

Non-residents carrying on a business or providing taxable goods or services within the United Kingdom must register. Other non-resident businesses may find it to their advantage to register. United Kingdom traders may find it to their advantage to register as taxable traders under the laws of other European countries in which they have business connections.

Registration

Registration involves completing a form that will be available, probably from September onwards, at Customs and Excise offices throughout the country. As far as possible, the necessary forms together with detailed instructions will be sent out to all known traders who may be liable. This will be supplemented by extensive newspaper and other advertising. Nevertheless, the obligation is on any trader who thinks he may be a taxable person to obtain a copy of the relevant form to be completed and to return it to the Customs and Excise. Registration periods will probably be staggered alphabetically or otherwise. For instance, traders whose business names begin with A, B or C may have to register by 1st November, 1972, and so on. Where a taxable business is set up after the deadline for initial registration or where the turnover of an existing business expands to make it registerable, the Customs and Excise will have to be notified within 10 days.

On registration the trader will be notified of his VAT registration number and of the address of the Customs and Excise office which will handle his affairs.

Amendment to Registration

There will be an obligation to notify the Customs and Excise whenever there is a change in the name, trading style or address of the business or when the owner or one of the owners of an unincorporated business changes his name or his private address. Changes in the composition of a partnership will also have to be notified. This will include cases where a sole trader takes in one or more partners or where, as a result of the death or retirement of all but one of the partners, a partnership business reverts to a sole proprietorship. Similarly a company which is a taxable person will have to notify changes in the address of its registered office, changes in its name or a change in its status from limited to unlimited liability or vice versa. There will be no need to notify changes in the share-holding or in the composition of the Board of Directors although the Customs and Excise will probably require to be notified if there is a change in the company secretary or other persons who act as the representative of the company for VAT purposes. Where a company is formed to take over a previously unincorporated business, there will have to be a notification. For income tax and corporation tax purposes such a transaction would be treated as the cessation of one business and the commencement of a new one subject to certain relieving provisions. For VAT purposes it may be treated as a carrying on of the same business under the same registration number (see Clause 25).

The Customs and Excise will also have to be notified if the business is closed down, if there is a bankruptcy or composition with creditors; or if a company is wound up or a receiver is appointed.

Accounts

Every taxable trader will have to keep accounts sufficient for him to calculate the amount of VAT payable by him or recoverable from the Customs and Excise in each accounting period. There is no prescribed form in which accounts must be kept but they must be open to audit by an officer of the Customs and Excise. The following are the minimum requirements.

Output tax

This will be a record of the VAT charged on all supplies of taxable goods or services and the application of taxable goods for personal use or use within an exempt trade.

Where a trader supplies goods to another trader he will be required to make out a tax invoice as described below. This will have to be recorded. The simplest procedure will be to have an extra column in the sales ledger.

Input Tax

This will be a record of the VAT charged on all taxable goods and services purchased by the trader and shown on the tax invoices received. Normally, the simplest way of recording this would be an extra column in the purchase ledger.

Tax Invoice

This will be issued in all cases where one trader supplies goods to another trader, and is the key to the mechanism. It will show the price of the goods, date of supply and the VAT. It will also probably have to show the supplier's VAT reference number which information will normally be printed on the form.

Tax Credit Note
This will show the same information as the tax invoice but
the transaction will be in reverse.

Quarterly Accounting
At the end of each quarter, or month in certain cases, the
trader will have to make a return to the Customs & Excise.
This will simply show the total output of the tax on sales less
the VAT re-credited on credit notes and the total input tax,
that is the total tax charge on tax invoices received less VAT
credited on tax credit notes received. The difference between
these figures will be the amount of VAT due to be paid. This
will be payable one month after the end of the accounting
period. Where the input tax exceeds the output tax for any
reason the Customs and Excise will make a reclaim also in
principle one month after the end of the accounting period.
Prompt repayment will obviously depend on prompt submis-
sion of returns by traders.

5. Timetable for Action

VAT comes into full force in April 1973. There are, however, a number of essential courses of action that should be taken before then. In this Chapter these are summarised.

ACTION NOW
Must you register?
Yes, if you expect to supply taxable zero rated goods and services to an annual value of £5000 or more. See Chapter 2.

Should you register?
Even if you qualify as a small trader it may be in your interests to register. See Chapter 2.

How do you register?
You should receive a circular from the Customs and Excise with full instructions in or around October. If you do not, press advertisements will advise you where you should apply for the necessary forms.

Are your goods and services exempt, zero rated or otherwise specially treated?
See Chapters 12 to 19.

Are some, but not all, of your supplies exempt?
If so, special procedures will be needed to allocate input tax. See Chapter 9.

Should a group of companies be registered as a single "taxable person" or should the group be divided?
See Chapters 2 and 11.

Should an individual trader or single company be divided into separate registered "taxable person"?
See chapter 2.

Are your accounting procedures geared for VAT?
It will be necessary to record separately both the tax charged out to customers and the input tax shown on invoices received from suppliers.

Are your staff trained in the implications of VAT?
Buy them extra copies of this book.

For the non-residents only. *Must you, or should you, register as a taxable person within the UK?*
This may be necessary or desirable if taxable supplies are bought in the UK and redelivered without being exported.

ACTION OCTOBER
Register in accordance with instructions that will be issued by the Customs and Excise. When allotted a VAT registration number ensure that this is printed on all invoice and credit note forms.

Re-check accounting procedures and start training. These must be fully operational by 1st April.

Study Customs and Excise regulations on points affecting the business. These should clear up any points of ambiguity. If they do not, or if you are not satisfied, you should seek guidance or make representations.

ACTION 1st APRIL
Ensure that all sales of taxable goods and services whether for cash or on invoice include the correctly calculated VAT.

Ensure that a record is maintained of all taxed invoices on supplies bought. In particular, obtain an invoice or receipt showing VAT even on cash purchases.

Ensure that accounting procedures are operational.

KEY TO SPECIAL TREATMENT

(See Chapters 12 to 14 for more information)

ACCOUNTANTS	Taxable
ADVERTISEMENTS (Newspapers & Periodicals)	Zero rated
ADVERTISEMENTS (other)	Taxable
AIR CONDITIONING (supplied to buildings)	Zero rated
AIR TRAVEL	Zero rated
ALCOHOL	Excise taxes plus VAT
ANIMALS	Zero rated if normally used for, or to produce, food, taxable otherwise
ARTISTS	Taxable
BANK CHARGES	Exempt
BANK INTEREST	Exempt
BANK NOTES	Zero rated on issue
BETTING	Exempt but subject to separate taxes
BOOKS	Zero rated
BUILDING CONSTRUCTION	Zero rated
BURIAL AND CREMATION	Exempt
CARAVANS	Mobile caravans taxable, large caravans zero rated
CARS	Taxable plus car tax

CIGARETTES	Taxable plus excise tax
COAL	Zero rated
COKE	Zero rated
CONFECTIONERY	Taxable
DENTISTS	Exempt
DOCTORS	Exempt
DRINK	Normally taxable. Alcoholic drinks also beer, excise taxes. Water is normally zero rated.
DRUGS AND MEDICINES	Zero rated only if supplied on prescription.
EDUCATION	Normally exempt
ELECTRICITY	Zero rated
ESTATE AGENTS	Taxable
EXPORTS	Zero rated
FINANCE	Exempt
FOOD	Zero rated with exceptions
FUEL AND POWER	Zero rated but oil fuels suffer excise tax.
GAS	Zero rated
GOLD	Bullion, and coins sold to authorised dealers, zero rated. Gold for manufacturing or numismatic coins taxable.
HEATING SUPPLIED TO BUILDINGS	Zero rated

HOTEL BUILDINGS	Taxable
HOUSES	Zero rated if new, exempt otherwise
INSURANCE	Exempt
INTEREST ON LOANS	Exempt
LAND	Exempt (Construction zero rated)
LAWYERS	Taxable
MANUFACTURERS	Taxable
MAPS	Zero rated
MEALS OUT	Taxable
MEDICINES	ZERO RATED only if supplied on prescription
MUSIC (printed)	Zero rated
MUSIC (performances)	Taxable
NEWS SERVICES	Zero rated
NEWSPAPERS	Zero rated
OIL	Zero rated but excise tax
PAINTING	Taxable
PERIODICALS	Zero rated
PETROL	Zero rated but excise tax
POSTAL SERVICES	Exempt (but *not* telephone or telex)
POWER	Zero rated

SCHOOL FEES	Normally exempt
RESTAURANT MEALS	Taxable
SECOND HAND GOODS	Taxable but there will be special rates
SERVICES	Taxable
SOLICITORS	Taxable
SOFT DRINKS	Taxable
SWEETS	Taxable
TELEPHONES	Taxable
TELEX	Taxable
THEATRE TICKETS	Taxable
TOBACCO	Taxable plus excise tax
TRAIN JOURNEYS	Zero rated
TRANSPORT	Zero rated except pleasure vehicles and trips.

6. Avoidance Rules and Enforcement

The general structure of VAT should now be clear. A trader who supplies taxable goods or services must charge VAT to his customer and must account for this VAT to the Customs and Excise as an output tax. If he supplies zero rated goods these are technically within the system but the output tax is zero. A month after the end of each accounting period he must pay over to the Customs and Excise the whole of the output tax he has charged his customers less the whole of the input tax charged to him on his purchases during the corresponding period. If the input tax exceeds the output tax for any reason, including the zero rating of some of the outputs, the Customs and Excise will pay a cash reclaim.

The real difficulties come in the definitions and the border lines between taxable, exempted and zero rated goods and services. These will be discussed in Part 3. Before coming to them there are a few small but important complications which will affect everybody.

Self Supply

Where a trader uses goods from his own stock for personal consumption there is a taxable transaction for VAT purposes. This covers the simple case where a retailer simply takes goods from his stock home for consumption by his family. He will be deemed to have sold the goods at the cost to him. He will have to account for VAT on the transaction (the Inland Revenue might also seek to levy income tax on the benefit in kind, but that is another matter).

Self supply is a much broader concept than this, and is one of two important anti-avoidance provisions in the Bill. It is defined in Schedule 2. Paragraph 1 of this Schedule deems there to be a taxable supply in cases "where goods acquired or produced by a taxable person in the course of a business...are applied to him to the personal use of himself or any other person". This catches gifts, including commercial samples. Schedule 3 sets out the rules for the determining of the price of goods which are self supplied. Paragraph 6 of that Schedule provides that the price shall be deemed to be the *cost* to the trader and not the arms length retail *price*. The trader does not therefore have to pay VAT on the profit he might have made when he actually sold the goods. In the case of a gift, if the cost is less than £10 its value shall be taken to be nil. This solves the problem for most commercial samples. It also appears to open the way for a trader to avoid VAT on his personal Christmas gifts by giving goods from his own stock provided that they cost less than £10. The VAT saving would remain even if the Inland Revenue cancelled out any income tax saving.

Paragraph 3 provides that where someone ceases to be a taxable person he shall for the purpose of his final accounting period be deemed to have supplied all his goods in stock to himself. This would cover the case of a trader whose turnover had dropped below £4000 per annum and claimed small trader exemption (see Chapter 2). This would prevent him stocking up the year's supply of goods while he was still taxable, claiming credit on the inputs and subsequently selling without VAT. Without such a provision it is easy to imagine ways in which an apparently small scale benefit could be multiplied systematically into large scale avoidance.

There is another potentially important case of self supply, This is where an exempt trader produces for his own use goods which he would otherwise have to buy and which would suffer VAT. The provision in Clause 6 simply gives the Treasury power to make orders. It is stated in the White Paper that an order will be made, effective from the start of the tax, covering stationery. Exempt traders, particularly banks and insurance companies, use a great deal of printing and stationery. If they were to buy these outside VAT would be charged on the invoice. This would not be creditable or recoverable. If there were no provision such traders may find it worthwhile to set up their own printing facilities. If they now do so the tax position will be the same as if they bought the stationery from outside.

The main reason for this provision is to prevent distortions of competition rather than to protect the Revenue. If banks and insurance companies were given a substantial inducement to print their own stationery their present suppliers would suffer. A situation might be created where existing printers had over-capacity, while their old customers were creating new capacity. Even if the outcome was for banks to buy up the business of printers the seller would be bargaining from weakness and would probably not get a fair price for the purchase.

Bankruptcy

Paragraph 2 of Schedule 2 provides that where a trader's goods are sold by a third party in order to set off a debt by a trader, the goods shall be treated as being supplied. This would cover repossessions or sales in the course of a bankruptcy. It is simply a legal provision to ensure what most people would regard as the common sense result.

Non-Deductible Inputs

Another necessary anti-avoidance provision gives the Customs and Excise power, by Order, to disallow the deduction of the input tax on certain purchases. This will apply where the purchases can be used for business or personal purposes. Orders will be introduced effective 1st April, 1973 disallowing credit of the input tax on the purchase of business cars and on expenditure on business entertaining except for the entertaining of foreign customers. Other categories may be added later if they prove to be necessary. The same effect could be achieved by treating the personal use of a self supply, but from an administrative and enforcement point of view it is probably better, where possible, to attack the problem at the earlier stage rather than the later stage.

If there is to be a blanket disallowance of the input tax on the purchase of business cars it goes too far, and over-corrects for any possible abuse. Cars are generally used for business purposes. Where they are also used for private purposes the Inland Revenue makes an assessment on the user. This is based on apportionment of the car between business and private use. The simplest solution would be for the Customs and Excise to liaise with the Inland Revenue (as the Bill gives them power to do) and to apply the same basis. Against this they might argue that they get their tax only on the purchase of the car while the Inland Revenue can make assessments during the whole period of the use. A business might take care to ensure that a car was used for exclusively business purposes during the first quarter and there would be no basis for a disallowance. Subsequently it might be used substantially or mainly for private purposes but the VAT credit would have already been granted. The answer to this is probably to make an interim assessment, perhaps on a standard 50/50 basis, and to make a retrospective adjustment at the end of each year.

An unfortunate side effect of disallowing input tax on cars would be to reduce quite substantially the very small advantage VAT would give to exports. Exports are zero rated, which is not *dramatically* significant as export customers do not at present pay purchase tax or other similar taxes. However, some small element of purchase tax was borne in the course of manufacture of export goods and there was no procedure for recovering this. Replacement of purchase tax by creditable VAT would, it was argued, remove this small export dis-incentive. It has been suggested that a country with VAT has about a 1½% competitive advantage over a country with purchase tax in the export market. On the whole purchase tax is not levied on goods bought by business, except in the case of goods which can be used equally by business or by private individuals. The most important category was cars and disallowing the credit in this specific case will almost eliminate this advantage.

Enforcement
The provisions described above are intended to prevent more obvious forms of avoidance. There are enabling provisions under which the Customs and Excise can issue Regulations. A detailed discussion of them seems out of place. I am also not discussing the enforcement procedures which are described in clauses 30—40 of the Bill and in Schedule 6. The general

reader can assume that VAT will be effectively enforced, that technical loopholes will be closed, and that those who attempt to evade payment of the tax will be prosecuted. Those who want further information can read the actual text of the Bill in Appendix 1. Anyone who thinks he has found a technical loophole may well be disappointed to find that it is closed by the amending of the Bill during its parliamentary stages or by the subsequent Regulations. From the point of view of an author the search for loopholes is automatically self-defeating. Merely to suggest a loophole in this book amounts to the certainty that it will be closed.

The extent of the powers taken seems excessive, especially for a tax which is in principle self-policing. This aspect of the tax has been widely criticised, particularly by lawyers and others concerned with the liberty of the subject. It may well be that the powers will be whittled down by the House of Commons.

7. Returns, Discounts and Bad Debts

Where goods are returned for credit, or where the purchaser negotiates a reduction in price on the grounds that the goods were not up to sample or for other reasons, the procedures will probably provide for a reversal of the original transaction. This aspect was covered in discussion papers but not (specifically) in the Bill or White Paper. If the purchaser is not a taxable person but is a private consumer or an exempt trader, the seller would simply treat the credit as an off-set against and a deduction from his sales in the accounting period. This would reduce the amount of VAT he has to pay over in that period. There would be no need to re-open the accounts for the previous period during which the goods were originally supplied. Where the purchaser was himself a taxable trader, the seller would have to issue a tax credit note giving the same information as the tax invoice. The seller would deduct the credit from his sales subject to output tax during the period in which the credit note was issued. Similarly, the purchaser would have to treat the credit as a reduction from his creditable tax inputs in the period in which the credit was granted.

The same procedure should apply on credits or discounts given by suppliers to purchasers for whatever reason. For instance, some businesses sell on the basis of quantity discounts which are calculated on aggregated purchases throughout the year. Obviously, the amount of the discount cannot be determined until the year is over. If a credit note is then issued, it would be treated as described above.

Such rules would be simple and logical. If a discount is given on a sales invoice, this is a reduction of the amount of the sale on which VAT is calculated. If a credit is given as a specific subsequent transaction, it is given on a credit note and there is also a credit for the corresponding amount of VAT. The seller treats this as a reduction of his output tax for that period and the buyer to whom the credit note is issued treats it as a reduction of his input tax for the same period.

The only possible complication would be if there had been a change in the rate of VAT between the original sale and the subsequent credit. This point was discussed in the consultative documents but there do not appear to be any special provisions. Unless such are made by Regulation, the credit will presumably be at the rate in force when the credit is made.

Destruction of Goods

Where goods are destroyed, there is no sale and no taxable transaction. Where the owner of the goods is a taxable person, he will, in effect, have recovered the tax on the input. There is no procedure for refunding tax to an exempt trader in these circumstances. The receipt of insurance compensation would constitute a taxable disposal and VAT would be due.

Bad Debts

There is to be no procedure for refunding VAT when a debt proves to be bad. If a trader sells goods for £100 plus £10 VAT he will be owed £110. His liability to account for the £10 will be based on the invoice. If he subsequently fails to collect the debt he will lose the whole of £110 and not be able to recover the £10 from the Customs and Excise. This is a practical matter of administration. It is the delivery rather than payment which is the taxable transaction and it is up to the trader and not the Customs and Excise to make sure that he gets his money. If refunds were permitted very careful policing would be necessary to ensure sales, followed by the writing off of the sale price as a bad debt was not being used as a procedure to evade the self supply and gift rules. It would also be necessary to make sure that the input credit was disallowed to the defaulting purchaser. All things considered the procedure suggested is probably the most practicable. Arguably if a trader thinks that a debt might be bad and that he would recover less than 9.09% in a bankruptcy, he might simply forgive the debt by issuing a credit note. This procedure could be blocked by regulations issued under Schedules 2 and 3.

Hire Purchase, Leasing and Credit

Interest is exempt from VAT. Where goods are sold on hire purchase the payments include an element of repayment of the purchase price and an element of interest. Paragraph 3 of Schedule D provides that VAT should only be levied on the *cash* price stated in the hire purchase agreement. It will, however, be payable immediately by the trader. The *interest* element in the price will be free of VAT.

Similarly, where goods are supplied subject to a discount for prompt settlement VAT is calculated as if prompt payment were in fact made and the discount in fact claimed regardless of what actually happens. If the full price without the discount is paid the excess escapes VAT on the grounds that it is really payment of interest. (Schedule 3 paragraph 4). Similarly any interest or other penalty charged by a trader on an overdue customers account would be treated as a payment for financial services and would on general grounds fall outside the scope of VAT.

Clause 5 (2) provides that a leasing transaction is to be treated as a supply of goods and not as a supply of services. Consistency would appear to require that VAT should only be charged on a cash price but there are no specific provisions for this. Regulations will appear in due course covering this point.

8. Transitional Arrangements and the Problems of Purchase Tax Paid Stocks

As from the first day of the new system consumers will bear the 10% VAT on all purchases of taxable goods and services. It will matter neither to them nor to the trader whether the goods were in stock before the start of the system. Goods which retail at £10 net of tax will cost £11 including tax. If the trader had the goods in stock prior to the start of the system he will not have borne any VAT on them. He will collect £1 from the customer and eventually pay this over to the Customs and Excise without any credit. He might later replace the same goods at a price of £7 plus 70p VAT. The 70p will be included in the price he pays to his own supplier. He will still charge the customer £11 including £1 VAT but at the end of the period he will only have to account for 30p to the Customs and Excise. In both cases the trader has *borne* no tax and the customer has *paid* a full tax. The only difference is the stage at which it is paid. There is no problem and the right result is given automatically.

The right result would *not* be given if the goods had previously been subjected to purchase tax. Purchase tax is collected at a wholesale level. If at the start of the system the retailer has goods on which purchase tax has been paid he could not credit this against the VAT payment. If the goods had previously been subjected to purchase tax at 20% of the wholesale price of £7 the price to the retailer would be £8.40 including £1.40 purchase tax, and the price to the customer would be £11.40 including the retailer's margin. The effect of the replacement of purchase tax with VAT would be to reduce the retail price by 40p. If the retailer had paid £8.40 including purchase tax on goods expecting to sell them for £11 with a profit of £3 he would find that not only did he have to sell at £11 against the price of his competitor who was buying new stock, he would have to pay £1 of this over to the Customs and Excise as VAT. This profit would be reduced from £3 to £1.60.

This is very similar to the problem that arises with purchase tax when there were downward reductions in rates. As explained below this will not be a problem with VAT. What normally happens with cars and other consumer durables is that these are bought from wholesalers on a sale or return basis in such a way that purchase tax only becomes payable when the goods are actually sold to the customer. In the meantime they are technically the property of the wholesaler and purchase tax when paid is at the rate applicable at the time of the retail sale. The Government's White Paper, and the Chancellor in his Budget speech, suggested that traders should in advance of the introduction of VAT make extensive use of such an arrangement. Retailers are strongly advised to act on this advice. Failure to do so could be very expensive. The goods concerned are as follows:

	Purchase tax groups
Furs and fur goods	1(b), 2(b), 8(a), 9(b)(i)
Jewellery (real or imitation), clocks and watches, and precious metal articles of personal adornment	4(a) and (b), 17
Domestic appliances and apparatus (except the non-electric non-gas bottom rate goods)	12(b) to (e)
Radio and television receivers, valves, loudspeakers	18
Musical instruments, gramophones	19(a) and (b)
Gramophone records	19(c)
Tape recorders/reproducers	19A(c)
Tapes and containers	19A(b) and (c)
Cameras, enlargers and projectors	24(a) and (b)
Road vehicles	27
Hair waving and hair drying machines	30(c)

For other goods on which turnover is rather more rapid these arrangements will be inappropriate. It is therefore proposed that on the goods *not* listed above purchase tax will be abolished a short time before the introduction of VAT on the 1st April, 1973. The time chosen will have to be designed to give retailers a chance to clear most of their purchase tax paid stocks and to build up new stocks in preparation for VAT. Whatever period is chosen there is bound to be some who will nevertheless be left with excess tax paid stocks. Other traders are going to be able to buy goods free of purchase tax and sell them on to customers free of VAT thus for a short time escaping both taxes. Astute customers aided and abetted by astute retailers will doubtless take advantage of the opportunity to build up their own stocks. This may be a bonanza. It is unlikely to be as extensive as the concession given in Holland where the tax-paid element was refunded. It has been suggested that the total loss due to falsely exaggerated claims exceeded £30 million.

A similar problem could arise if the rates of excise duty on alcoholic drinks, tobacco, matches and mechanical lighters is reduced somewhat to allow for the fact that VAT will be chargeable on these goods in addition. Again it is proposed that the date of change will be so arranged to enable people to reduce or run down stocks. This could create problems for the better class of wine merchant accustomed to carry an extensive and rather slow-moving stock. They should start planning well ahead and make the maximum use of bonded warehouse facilities. The problem does not arise with hydrocarbon oils as these are to be zero rated for VAT.

Changes in VAT Rates
Although the rate of VAT will probably initially be 10%, the Chancellor is keeping his options open and the initial rate may be anywhere in the range 7½% to 12½%. The rate may be changed in subsequent Budgets or by the use of the "regulator" (now more powerful) between Budgets. However, with VAT, there is in general no problem of losses on tax-paid stocks as there is with purchase tax. Assume that a retailer had before the 1972 Budget bought a camera at a wholesale price of £100 plus purchase tax of 45% making £145 in all. He hoped to

make a gross profit of £30 by selling to the customer at £175. On 21st March, 1972 the rate of purchase tax on cameras was reduced to 25%. The customer expected an immediate reduction in the price of £20 and unless the price is cut to £155 (£100 wholesale price plus £25 purchase tax plus £30 retailer's margin) the customer will either wait or go elsewhere to a shop which acquires its stock after the change. The retailer has already paid £145 and as a result of the change he will find his margin on the transaction squeezed from his expected £30 to £10. The situation is not symmetrical. When purchase tax goes up customers do not expect an immediate increase and most retailers find that they are forced to advertise "pre-Budget prices while stocks last". In practice arrangements are usually made to avoid or minimise this risk.

With VAT, the risk for *taxable* traders does not exist. The retailer buys the camera for £100 plus £10 VAT. His selling price is £143 including £13 VAT. He credits the £10 charged on his input against the £13 he has collected from his customer and pays over £3 to the Customs and Excise at the end of the quarter. This leaves him with his £30 margin as before. If the rate of VAT goes down to 5%, he will charge his customer £136.50 including £6.50 VAT. However, he has a £10 tax credit and can recover the odd £3.50 from the Customs and Excise. It does not matter in principle whether the credit was claimed in a previous period or is due for offset in the current period. The system is self-correcting and the Customs and Excise themselves bear the brunt of the change. They collect at one stage or another 10% on all retail sales made up until the date of the change and 5% on all retail sales made after the date regardless of whether the goods were in the productive process at the time.

On the other hand, when rates go up there is neither a windfall gain to the retailer nor is it possible to advertise "pre-Budget prices while stocks last". If VAT rises to 20% the retail price of the camera would immediately be increased to £156 including £26 VAT. On the sale, the retailer would have to account for £26 output tax and would only receive a credit of £10 input tax. He would actually have to pay over £16 to the Customs and Excise. When he replaced the camera he would have to pay his supplier £120 including £20 VAT. This increase would be matched because of the credit by a reduction to £6 in the amount of VAT he himself would have to pay over.

The effect on individual transactions is given by way of illustration. From an administrative point of view, all the retailer would have to do is to account for output tax at 10% on all sales up to the date of the change and at 20% on all sales after the date of the change. He would then deduct from the total his input taxes as the sum of money shown on the invoice without being directly concerned as to the rate at which these taxes were imposed.

There is still a gain to the *private consumer* (or exempt trader) in buying before an increase or refraining from buying before an anticipated decrease in the rate of VAT, but the retailer as such will not have to take a view on his stock policy.

VAT at Multiple Rates

The United Kingdom has decided, in common with the Scandinavian countries, to have a single rate VAT subject to zero rates and exemption. The five EEC countries already operating VAT impose the tax at multiple rates. A description of their systems is given in Chapter 26 and there is a discussion of the economic arguments for single and multiple rates in Chapter 23. I just want to give a brief description of how multiple rates work and to show that multiple rates are consistent with the concept of VAT.

A trader who sells different categories of goods and services subject to different rates would obviously have more work to do, He would have to show the categories separately on the invoices and make a separate calculation of VAT due. This is simple enough for a large manufacturer but somewhat complicated for the retailer carrying on a cash business.

The rate ultimately borne by the consumer is the rate applicable to the product he actually buys. Suppose the product bears tax at 20% while some of the components going into its production bear tax only at 10%. The following illustration shows what happens. It will be seen that the tax paid over by the actual final seller is equal to 20% on his own value added plus the extra 10% on those inputs previously taxed at only 10%. This is the "catching up phenomenon".

Sales (net of VAT)	6,000
Purchase (net of VAT)	4,000
"Value Added"	2,000
Output tax £6,000 at 20%	1,200
Input tax £4,000 at 10%	400
VAT payable	£ 800

Note that the trader pays over VAT of £800 on a value added of £2,000. This can work in reverse. The second example is what happens when the inputs have been taxed at 20% and the final output only at 10%. It will be seen that the final trader gets a refund of £200 even though his own value added amounts to £2,000.

(Sales and purchases as before).	
Output tax £6,000 at 10%	600
Input tax £4,000 at 20%	800
VAT *refundable*	£200

Again each trader does not have to worry himself about these details. As before, all he does is to add up total VAT due on his own sales during the quarter at whatever rate and to deduct the input of tax again at whatever rate. It will be seen that the principle and the underlying simplicity of the credit mechanism is maintained in spite of the multiple rates. The experience of other countries suggests that the operation of multiple rates adds about 50% to the cost of administration. The proportionate extra administrative load on retailers handling goods in different categories might be higher.

9. Partially Exempt Traders

An exempt trader does not have to charge VAT on his sales but cannot recover VAT charged to him on his input. A special problem arises where a trader supplies some goods or provides some service which is exempt while other goods or services are taxable or zero rated. (For this purpose taxable and zero rated goods and services can be considered together as the supply of either makes the trader eligible for recovery of his input tax.) In principle input tax will be recoverable only to the extent to which it refers to taxable or zero rated outputs and will not be recoverable to the extent to which it relates to exempt outputs. The most important cases are going to concern finance and insurance (see Chapter 16), but ophthalmic opticians, dental technicians who do other work, and pharmaceutical chemists may also find themselves involved.

There are going to have to be rules for allocating inputs. This is one of the most difficult points on which the draft legislation is not specific and where we will have to wait for a detailed Regulation. Clause 3 (3) (b) states that only such part of input tax which is attributable to taxable supplies may be deducted. Clause 3 (4) states that the Commissioners shall make regulations for securing a "fair and reasonable" attribution of input tax to taxable supplies and goes on to say that they make different provisions for different circumstances, or for different descriptions of goods or services. The regulations may also "contain such incidental and supplementary provisions as appears to the Commissioners necessary or expedient."

This all tells us very little. Paragraph 18 of the White Paper gives rather more guidance. It suggests that the normal rule will be for the input tax to be apportioned in the same ratio that taxable (or zero rated) supplies bear to total supplies. If, therefore, in an accounting period a trader has taxable sales of £10,000 (output tax £1,000) zero rated sales of £1,000 (no output tax) and exempt sales of £6,000 he would only be entitled to deduct seven tenths of his input taxes. If his taxed inputs were £12,000 (input tax £1,200) he will only be entitled to deduct £840 of this. As his output tax was £1,000 he would have to pay over to the Customs and Excise the sum of £160 even though his *total* input tax actually exceeded his output tax by £200.

In practice, this simple rule will seldom be realistic and detailed Regulations will have to be made for each trade. Regardless of the detail into which these Regulations go, it is at least a racing certainty that their interpretation will cause a lot of disputes between taxpayers and tax gatherers and will occupy a great deal of the time of the Courts. It will be open to a trader with some exempt activities to divide his business into two separate divisions. As explained in Chapter 2 a single trader, including a single company can be split into separate divisions which are separately registered as "taxable persons" and which keep separate VAT accounts. At least for activities within the United Kingdom the divisions and grouping for VAT purposes need not bear any relationship to the structure of a group of companies for accounting or corporation tax purposes. If a merchant bank wishes to hive off its taxable activities from its exempt activities it can do so without forming a separate subsidiary.

Where exempt activities are hived off from taxable and zero rated activities separate accounts will be kept and inputs will be allocated between the two classes. Obviously, the Customs and Excise will watch carefully to ensure that tax inputs are not wrongly allocated to the taxable activities when they should really belong to the exempt activities. If the regulations covering a particular situation apply an arbitrary set of rules such as the simple apportionment of turnover discussed above the trader affected will have to decide whether this arbitrary answer will be better or worse from his point of view than a strict accounting. He may find himself better off by actually keeping all his activities under the same hat and accepting a national apportionment. On the other hand, if the basis is not in his favour he should consider hiving off the activity into separate accounting units and keeping strict and separate records.

It has been suggested that in the case of partially exempt traders there will be a provisional quarterly accounting on a "rule of thumb" basis supplemented by an annual accounting following which adjustments may be made. Because more detailed information will be needed for the activities of such traders, they will probably be allotted a quarterly accounting cycle so that the end of one of the quarters coincides with the end of their financial year. Normally, the cycle will be selected by the Customs and Excise to spread their own work level and will not necessarily coincide with the financial year.

10. Capital Investment

Capital equipment is subject to VAT in the normal way. This is necessary for consistency. In the normal case where the capital equipment is purchased by a taxable trader the input tax will be credited as usual. There is no need to differentiate between input on capital purchases and input on revenue purchases. There is, therefore, in the United Kingdom to be no special problem of capital investment and VAT.

A trader might, in a typical quarter, have sales of £250,000 of which the output tax is £25,000 and be making taxed purchases of £150,000 on which the input tax was £15,000. One month after the end of such a typical quarter he would have to pay £10,000 to the Customs and Excise. If the trader is building a new factory it may well happen that in the course of one quarter he takes delivery of plant and machinery at a cost of £500,000 plus VAT on the invoice of £50,000, making £550,000. In this particular quarter there will be output tax of £25,000 as usual but input taxes including that on the capital purchases of £65,000, and the trader will be able to make a reclaim of £40,000 from the Customs and Excise.

There are provisions by which traders such as exporters and those supplying mainly zero rated goods and services can opt for monthly accounting to speed up the repayment. We shall have to await the regulations to see whether this is to be a once for all option or only exercisable for a certain minimum period of time. The trader we have just described is normally a net payer of VAT and would therefore normally prefer a quarterly accounting period. We do not yet know whether he can switch temporarily to monthly accounting to make a faster reclaim of the VAT content in his machinery purchases. This point may not be very important in practice because of the length of credit normally associated with capital purchases.

The solution chosen in the United Kingdom and in most other countries is a simple and practical one. The historical account of taxes on value added given in Chapter 26 shows this is by no means the only possible solution. Indeed, from the point of view of an economist trying to construct a logical tax which really fell on some true concept of "value added", the right thing to do would be to have the purchasing business bear the tax in the first instance and only to claim the credits over a period of years on the same kind of basis as depreciation.

Fortunately in most countries simplicity has triumphed over logic. The one exception, predictably enough, was France. Until new regulations were brought in in early 1972 a French business with an excess of input tax over output tax could not normally claim an actual repayment. One exception was when the reclaim arose from the zero rating of exports. In other cases the so-called "buffer rule" applied and the excess credits could only be carried forward until they could be used up. This imposed a heavy financial burden on expanding businesses. In particular, new businesses would have to bear the full VAT content on the machinery they purchased without any immediate reclaim. A full reclaim would only be made once the total of sales less purchases equalled the cost of the machine. This would take a year or two at least and it was estimated that at one time the result of the buffer rule was that French business was effectively making an interest-free loan of some 3 billion francs to the French Government. The buffer rule has now been amended. For financial reasons, only one quarter of excess credits outstanding at the end of 1971 are to be reimbursed. The balance will probably be paid off over five years, subject to the right of traders to offset them against any future liabilities during that period. From 1972 onwards there are to be full reclaims on new capital purchases and the much criticised buffer rule will gradually be phased out.

Sales of second hand machinery will be subject to VAT in the normal way and the purchasing business will be able to claim a creditable input tax. This again has a simple and consistent rule on the assumption that the only people likely to handle second hand machinery are taxable persons. There are special problems with second hand consumer goods and these are discussed in Chapter 19.

11. VAT and Cash Flow

The basis of accounting periods for VAT will be such that the trader would normally be in pocket. Traders who expect to make net *payments* will choose three monthly accounting periods. Those who will normally make a *reclaim* (exporters and suppliers of zero rated goods and services) will be able to choose a monthly accounting period. The implications are simple enough, but they might be worth examining in a little more detail. First, take the simple case of a trader who has sales of £2,000 per month and no taxed inputs. If he trades for cash he will collect from his customers £200 per month on behalf of the Customs and Excise. If he has an accounting period ending 30th June he will collect £200 each in April, May and June, and at the end of June he will have in his custody £600 which he owes to the Customs and Excise. He will actually pay this at the end of July by which time he will have collected another £200. Immediately before he sends his cheque, he will have £800 in hand and immediately after he will have £200 in hand. Assuming that cash comes in steadily and regularly he will have the use of, on average, £500 of the Government's money.

There are two ways of looking at this. For the normal trader who operates on overdraft but who has no difficulty in negotiating as big an overdraft as he needs, it is simply a saving of interest. Assuming his bank overdraft costs 10% per annum, he saves £50 per annum (pre-tax income) on a turnover of £24,000. A trader who is harder pressed for liquidity might feel that he has been given a £200 float which he can regard as permanent capital in his business — so long as he goes on trading. He must not make the mistake of forgetting that he will have money to pay at the end of the quarter but he may take care to organise his other periodical cash fluctuations so that they fit neatly in with the VAT fluctuations.

Now consider a similar trader who sells not for cash but credit. He will still have also to pay £600 at the end of July in respect of goods invoiced during April, May and June, but he will now have to wait for his money until his own customers pay him. If his customers pay on the last day of the month following invoice, he will receive £2,200 (including £200 on account of April VAT) at the end of May and £200 VAT at the end of June and July in respect of sales in May and June. The last payment will exactly coincide with his own payment to the Customs and Excise. He will have £400 in hand just before he pays the Customs and Excise. On 31st July he will receive another £200 and pay £600 leaving him with exactly nothing in hand on 1st August. His average float works out at £200. He has £200 for the whole of June, £400 for the whole of July and nothing for the whole of August, and so on for the corresponding months of the other three quarterly accounting periods. If he gave longer credit than this he would actually be out of pocket for part of the cycle.

If we vary the assumptions so that the trader has sales of £1,500, the whole situation becomes rather more sensitive to credit terms. In this case, the trader will have to pay £150 at the end of July for net VAT of £50 in each month. If both his purchases and his sales were for cash he would have a maximum of £200 and a minimum of £50 on hand. If he bought for cash but gave one month's credit to his own customers, he would vary from £150 out of pocket to all square. If, however, his suppliers gave *him* credit he could find himself materially better off.

The trader buying taxed inputs and selling zero rated outputs would be able to recover £150 at the end of each month. If he bought for cash and had a three month accounting period, he would, at the end of July, have borne £600 of recoverable VAT. He would then receive £450 in respect of the three months April to June. He would be out of pocket a minimum of £150 and a maximum of £600. To avoid this, he would opt for a monthly accounting period and would be out of pocket for a minimum of £150 and a maximum of £300. If his suppliers gave him credit permitting him to pay at the end of the month following invoice, he would be exactly all square at all times in respect of VAT. If his suppliers gave him longer credit, he would be in pocket. Note that in this case as there is no VAT on the output it is immaterial to the calculation what credit terms the supplier gives against his own customer. (In practice these credit terms for the goods themselves are far more important than the credit on the 10% VAT content. The object of this Chapter is merely to show the *changes* introduced into cash flow calculations by VAT).

It will be interesting to see whether it is possible for groups of companies to register subsidiaries or divisions which supply zero rated goods and services on separate taxable persons. The obvious example is an export subsidiary. The manufacturing division would then invoice the export division during April charging VAT on the invoice. The manufacturing division would only have to account for this VAT on July 31st while the export division could reclaim the VAT on May 31st.

Take the example of a group of companies with total inputs of £110,000 per month and total outputs of £200,000 per month of which £50,000 were exports. If the group were a single "taxable person" net VAT of £4,000 per month, or £12,000 at the end of each quarter, would be due. (Whether this leaves the group in credit or not depends on credit terms). An export company might be registered as a separate "taxable person" and opt for monthly accounting. The rest of the group would invoice exports to the export company, which would then invoice them on to customers. The position would then be as follows:

In April the manufacturing group sells goods to the export company for £55,000 including VAT. Export company exports to customers for £50,000 zero rated. Ignore the internal financial transaction — it is irrelevant to the group whether and when it is settled.

The manufacturing group has sales of £200,000 including the sales to the export company, and must account for £20,000 VAT less £11,000 input tax making £9,000 payable 31st July.

The export company has input tax of £5,000, which it can reclaim on 31st May, 1972.

In May the manufacturing group incurs a liability to pay £9,000 on 31st July. The export company can create a reclaim for 30th June.

In June the manufacturing group incurs a liability to pay £9,000 and the export company creates a reclaim, both due on 31st July.

In summary

	No Separate Export Co. Payments to C. & E.	Separate Payments to C. & E.	Export Co. Reclaim from C. & E.	Relative Cash in Hand
May 31	NIL	NIL	(5,000)	5,000
June 30	NIL	NIL	(5,000)	10,000
July 31	12,000	27,000	(5,000)	NIL

This could be profitable. It may not be permitted when the Regulations are issued.

12. Zero Rated Transactions

In the United Kingdom VAT is to be levied at a flat rate, probably 10%. The system will thus differ from and be simpler than the multi-rate systems found in most EEC countries. However, certain transactions will be exempted from the tax while others will be zero rated. The vitally important distinction between exemption and zero rating was explained in Chapter 3. In this Chapter and the next we examine the proposed categories which will receive one or the other of these special treatments.

Inevitably this is the subject on which there is most scope for controversy and the greatest likelihood of changes both during the debates on this year's Finance Bill and in future years. The experience of SET and of other countries also indicates that most of the disputes, court cases and opportunities for altering the incidence of the tax will be based on the exact meaning of some of the definitions.

The zero rated goods and services are set out in Schedule 4 to the Bill and the exemptions in Schedule 5. As the text of the Bill is reproduced as Appendix 2, I will not repeat the exact definitions here. I propose in each case to describe the provisions, to discuss possible difficulties, and where it seems relevant or interesting to explain what happens in other countries. In Chapter 14 I discuss a number of categories which are *not* given special treatment in the United Kingdom, but which are in certain other countries adopting VAT.

ZERO RATED CATEGORIES IN SCHEDULE 4
Group 1 Food and drink
Food, including animal feeding stuffs, seeds and live food animals will in general be zero rated. The exceptions to this

general rule which will be taxed in the normal way are set out in Schedule 4 Group 1. Particularly note that there are "items over-riding the exceptions" which *will* be zero rated. Very broadly, the exceptions fall into three categories. First of all, meals taken in restaurants, hotels and other catering establishments will be taxable. This will apply to the whole cost of the meal and not just to the service element. The restaurant, will, of course, be able to buy its food on a zero rated basis but as there will be no input tax there will be no credit. The full 10% will have to be added on to the cost of the meal as an output tax. To the extent to which there are input taxes on non-food (or non-exempted food) purchases, there will be credit in the normal way.

The private citizen eating in a restaurant will have 10% added to the total cost of his meal. This does not necessarily mean that the total cost of such meals will rise by this amount as SET, a particularly heavy charge on restaurants, will be abolished at the same time as the introduction of VAT. In addition, restaurants previously had to pay and absorb into their costs, purchase tax on certain foods and drink and some of their equipment. This will now be replaced by a creditable VAT on the input.

Where a restaurant meal is paid for by a trader who is a taxable person under VAT, the VAT element in the cost of the meal would normally be a creditable tax on an input. However, Clause 3 (6) of the Bill gives the Treasury power to disallow certain payments for the purpose of input taxes. They have already announced that they will use this power to disallow expenditure on business entertaining, other than of overseas customers. In other words, the cost of normal business entertaining will not only be disallowed as a deduction for income tax or corporation tax, but the VAT element will not be recoverable. Where overseas customers are entertained it will be important to keep the receipt for the purpose of VAT credit and of a tax deduction.

The rule governing the disallowance of business entertaining was first introduced by a Labour Government and was attacked by the Conservative Party at that time as a piece of political vindictiveness. It may seem odd that the rule has not only been maintained by a Conservative Government but has been extended to the new VAT.

The second group of exceptions to the rule that food is zero rated are what might be called luxury foods of the type that were in any case caught by purchase tax. These include (for example) icecream, chocolates, sweets and confectionery, soft drinks, potato crisps, and salted peanuts. Obviously, there are going to be problems of definition. Chocolate biscuits are taxable, but chocolate covered cakes are not. If you like orange juice for breakfast you will escape VAT by buying oranges and squeezing them yourself. Orange juice in cans or bottles will be subjected to VAT. The old case involving the Savoy Hotel, where it was decided that the squeezing of oranges in an hotel constituted a "manufacturing process" for purchase tax purposes presumably still stands. It is now irrelevant in its context, as *all* food supplied by the Savoy will be subject to VAT

Pet foods will also be subject to VAT. Doubtless the pet food manufacturers will attempt to respond to this challenge by selling canned meat for human consumption, but described in the advertisement as "and for your doggie friend".

The third category which will be liable to VAT is alcoholic drinks. In the Schedule, they are lumped together with "other manufactured beverages" but in one respect they merit special treatment. This is because such drinks are already subject to excise taxes at very high rates. There are in principle two ways of dealing with this situation. One is to say that because they bear these specific duties they should be granted exemption or zero rating. The other is to subject them to VAT and to make a downward adjustment in the excise taxes to compensate. In general terms the latter procedure is simpler as it avoids the need for special treatment. Any such adjustment can only be approximate. The ultimate burden of VAT is based on the final selling price to the consumer. The alcohol duties are all specific duties based on alcohol content. The excise duties on a bottle of spirits depends on its alcoholic content. VAT would depend on the quality, and also on the retail margin. A cut in duty of a size which would be exactly replaced by the VAT yield over spirits as a whole would tend to reduce the tax burden on and price to the consumer of a cheap proprietary gin bought by the dozen at the keenest available discount. It could quite materially increase the tax on, and the price of, a fine malt whisky or a Grande Champagne cognac. This might also be true of the difference between the discount shop with a low markup and the wine merchant who makes a higher margin but who carries a comprehensive stock, advises, delivers and gives long credit. On the other hand the high-service retailer will benefit from the ending of SET which as Chapter 25 shows, discriminated against such businesses. The difference would be even more noticeable with wines. The present UK system of duties only discriminates between wines imported in casks and wines imported in bottles. While this puts a slightly higher *absolute* tax on chateau bottled wines, there is a much higher *relative* tax content on cheap Algerian hooch than there is on the finest Premier Cru. VAT will, to some extent, increase the relative cost of quality.

There is, of course, no guarantee that the introduction of VAT will in fact be matched by a corresponding reduction in the special excise taxes but the Government appears to recognise that this would be a net increase in the total tax burden on alcoholic drinks. It can therefore be assumed that if next year there is no corresponding reduction there would have been an increase had VAT not been introduced. The only real argument in favour of zero rating on the alcoholic drink is that there would then be no need to include it as an exception from the general category. However, as soft drinks are treated as an exception the method chosen is probably the simplest. One point is that where the purchase of alcoholic drinks amounts to a creditable tax input (which means in practice when drinks are bought for overseas customers) VAT is creditable while correspondingly higher rates of excise duty would not be. The implications of this are discussed again in connection with fuel oil. The cost of wine bought in restaurants will be less if there is a creditable VAT: otherwise full excise duty *PLUS* VAT would be borne.

In general, most European countries do impose VAT on food although in general at a reduced rate. There is a tradition of tax-free food in the United Kingdom going back to the days of the Corn Laws. We have always preferred to protect our farmers by subsidies while European countries have tended instead to tax imported food. There are no very strong economic arguments in favour of one method or the other. However, to have imposed VAT on food in the United Kingdom would have made the package much more difficult to sell politically. The importance attached to the cost of food as a component in the cost of living is disproportionate to its statistical significance in the modern world. It probably dates back to the early days of the Labour Movement when wages were really at a subsistence level and the price of bread had a significance second only to the level of money wages.

The argument that increases in the cost of food particularly hit the lower paid and pensioners and that it is therefore necessary to exclude them from tax has no validity, as explained in Chapter 23. It would have been perfectly possible to include food in VAT for the sake of simplicity. The extra revenue collected could then have been applied to compensating increases in cash social benefits and in personal tax allowances. This strategy would have been economically sound but perhaps politically unwise. It was applied successfully in Denmark where the introduction of VAT corresponded with a substantial restructuring of direct taxation. Once the public gets used to VAT it may, in fact, be found advisable to broaden the base.

No other European country zero rates or even exempts foods in general. In France certain basic foodstuffs are taxed at the lowest rate (7.5%) and others at the intermediate rate (17.60%) as compared with the full rate of 23%. Oddly, chocolate is included (alongside bread) in the lowest rate category while fruit juice, cider and wine benefit from the intermediate rate. These are *excluded* from the general zero rate treatment in the United Kingdom. Germany applied the reduced rate (5.5% as compared with 11%) in the case of meat, fish, milk and other dairy products, eggs, fruit, coffee, tea, margarine, sugar and water. The Netherlands applies the reduced 4% rate to potatoes, vegetables, fruit, dairy products, meat, fish, bread, coffee, tea and water.

Germany specifically exempts deliveries of mothers' milk (and preserved human blood) and services connected therewith. The Netherlands exempts deliveries of food and drink by non-profit organisations such as old people's homes. These, however are not very far reaching and do not seriously encroach on the general principle of the taxability of food.

Group 2 Water

Group 2 of the Fourth Schedule zero rates the supply of water other than distilled water or water supplied in connection with non-zero rated foodstuffs. This provision seems .to call for little comment. Sweden and Denmark exempt, rather than zero rate, the supply of water by waterworks. France and Germany, as remarked above, include water alongside essential foodstuffs in the lowest rate category.

Group 3 Books

Group 3 zero rates books, booklets, brochures, pamphlets, leaflets, newspapers, journals, periodicals, children's picture books and painting books, music (printed, duplicated or manuscript), maps, charts and topographical plans. The zero rating extends to covers, cases and other articles supplied with the other items but not separately accounted for. This is a far reaching concession which appears to cover most of the categories. It goes a little further than the concessions in other countries.

It is specifically provided that plans or drawings for industrial, architectural, engineering, commercial or similar purposes will *not* be zero rated. This makes sense. Such designs normally enter into the cost of production and where supplied to a taxable person would constitute a creditable tax on an input. Where they were supplied to an export customer they would be zero rated on general export grounds. The question of tax would only arise on plans and drawings supplied to a private individual. There would be difficulties of allocation if a kit of parts to assemble a car were taxable while the instructions on how to assemble were not.

France and Germany exempt, rather than zero rate, newspapers and periodicals. Denmark zero rates newspapers which appear at least once a week but not other magazines and books. The Netherlands zero rates newspapers sold on subscription.

Group 4 Newspapers

Newspapers and other periodicals are to be zero rated in respect of their advertising revenue as well as their sales revenue. This does not apply to television and other forms of advertising. This is of no concern to the *business* advertiser. It does not matter to him whether he advertises in a newspaper and is not invoiced with VAT or whether he advertises on television, has a 10% VAT added to his invoice and claims a credit. There will be a real benefit to individuals who use a newspaper's small advertisements but who are unlikely to advertise on television. From a practical point of view there is the advantage that a newspaper will not have to allocate its taxable inputs in the way described in Chapter 9.

There is another practical advantage. If a foreign trader who is not a taxable person within the United Kingdom buys advertising space in a United Kingdom journal, he does not have to consider the question of whether this is an "export of services" (see Chapter 22).

This concession appears to have no exact parallel in other European countries.

In France a reduction of VAT may be obtained by concession for advertisements in French journals which circulate abroad.

Group 5 News services

Logically enough the supply of news services is zero rated. The concession does not apply to photographs. Where such services are supplied to newspapers themselves this simply avoids the administrative problem of collecting the tax from the news service and refunding it to the newspaper. As with advertisements, it avoids the problem of allocation that would arise if a newspaper itself supplied the news service. Where a news service is supplied direct to the public (which in practice means news tapes to clubs, financial news services to stockbrokers and others, and services in connection with racing information) these are in a sense competitive with newspapers and it is probably right that they should be afforded the same treatment.

France exempts such services. No other countries appear to give special treatment.

Group 6 Fuel and Power

All fuels will be zero rated. This includes solid fuels, such as coal and coke, gases of all kinds, petrol and other hydrocarbon oils, methylated spirits used as fuel and electricity. It also extends to heat and air conditioning where these are supplied as services to residential or other buildings.

Hydrocarbon oils are already subjected to high rates of excise duty. Most business consumers would prefer that VAT were substituted for at least a part of this excise duty. (Compare the treatment of alcohol discussed above). This would mean that this part of the duty would be offset against the VAT due from their own customers, with the reduction of possible percentage effect and a clear, if small, advantage to exporters. The VAT element could also be recovered by transport undertakings most of which will also be zero rated (see below Group 9). It might, however, be difficult to give different treatment to different forms of fuel which is no doubt the reason for this at first sight odd provision. The case for protecting the domestic coal industry was never a very strong one. The "national security" part of the argument has surely been proved invalid by the events of earlier this year and is in any case being bypassed by the discovery of oil and natural gas in the North Sea.

Denmark exempts the supply of gas and electricity (and of water as referred to above) in connection with the renting of houses and rooms. Sweden zero rates electrical power, gas and other fuels for heating or for generating power. (This contrasts with the *exemption* of water supply by waterworks). France subjects gas and electricity to the intermediate rate. The Netherlands imposes the reduced rate of 4% on fuels in general and on the provision of heating.

Group 7 Construction of Buildings etc

The construction of buildings and the sale either of a freehold interest or of a leasehold for more than 21 years is zero rated. The implications of this are discussed in more detail in Chapter 18.

Group 8 Exports

As in all other countries, exports are zero rated. The

procedure is explained in Chapter 20. The special problem of definition for international transactions in services is discussed in Chapter 22.

Group 9 Transport
The provision of transport services is in general zero rated. This includes the supply, repair or maintenance of ships of 15 tons and over and aircraft of a weight of 18,000 lbs. or over provided that they are not designed or adapted for use for recreation or pleasure.

Group 10 Caravans
This group exempts "caravans exceeding the limits of size for the time being permitted for the use of trailers on roads". This is designed to assimilate the treatment of *residential* caravans with house building and purchase: see Chapter 18.

Group 11 Gold
The supply of gold bullion and the supply of gold coins by an authorised dealer in gold to another such dealer is zero rated. This means that where gold changes hands for what are essentially monetary purposes there is a zero rating. This is part of the general treatment of financial services discussed in Chapter 16.

The sale of gold coins other than to another authorised dealer *will* be subject to VAT. This would apply in the case of a sale to a collector. The general treatment of antiques and collectors' items is discussed in Chapter 19. It is provided that Section 12 (3) of the Act shall not apply to gold coins. This is the sub-section exempting zero rated goods from VAT at the point of importation. It seems therefore that gold coins could be subject to VAT at importation. This would have no significance if the purchase was by, or if the coins were subsequently sold to, an authorised dealer in gold. The tax *would* apply to an individual who imported gold coins.

Group 12 Bank Notes
The issue by a bank of a bank note is zero rated. Presumably the purchase of such notes by a bank from a printer would be a taxable transaction but the bank could recover this tax.

Group 13 Drugs and Medicines Supplied on Prescription

These are zero rated provided that they are dispensed by a registered pharmaceutical chemist on prescription from a registered doctor or dentist. The purchase of medicines other than on prescription will be subject to VAT. The supply of goods to a chemist will therefore be a taxable transaction. VAT will be added to the invoice. Some medicines are available without prescription. Their supply will be zero rated if they are actually supplied on a prescription but taxable if they are not. It would not therefore be possible to make a distinction at earlier stages. Depending on their profit margins the extent to which their business consists of filling prescriptions, some chemists may find themselves normally in the position of making a VAT reclaim. If they calculate that they will be in this position, they should consider opting for a one month payment period instead of a three month payment period. This would speed up their payments and improve their cash flows but against this must be set any additional administrative burden. (See Chapter 11).

Sweden also zero rates medicines delivered upon prescriptions or sold to hospitals but other countries appear to make no general provisions.

13. Exempted Transactions

The exemptions are set out in Schedule 5 of the Draft Bill. As explained in Chapter 13, exemption is less favourable than zero rating in that the exempt trader cannot claim a recovery of the VAT borne on his own taxable input.

Group 1 Land
This group exempts "the grant, assignment or surrender of any interest in or right over, land or of any licence to occupy land" with certain exceptions. This provision has to be studied in association with the *zero rating* of buildings and construction, and is discussed in Chapter 18.

It is specifically provided that the short term provision of accommodation, for instance in hotels or boarding houses, the granting of camping facilities, car parking facilities or game or fishing rights are *not* exempt and are subject to VAT in the normal way.

Group 2 Insurance
Insurance is exempt. The implications of this are studied in Chapter 16.

Group 3 Postal Services
The conveyance of postal packets by the Post Office and ancilliary services is exempt. The exemption does not extend to telephone, telegram and telex services which will be subject to VAT. This will add 10% to the cost of private telephone bills and to the cost of private telegrams. Most business users of telecommunications will not be affected as they will be able to offset the VAT content in the cost of these services against the tax payable on their taxable

outputs. Financial institutions are important users of telecommunications. Where they are exempt they will simply have to absorb the extra cost. To the extent to which they supply their services to business users, there will be a "sandwich effect". The business will have to pay more for financial services because of the element of VAT. Because the providers of the services are themselves exempted and there is no VAT element in the invoice, the indirectly borne tax will not be eligible as a credit. The sandwich effect is discussed in more detail in Chapter 3 and the special problems of financial and insurance services in Chapter 16.

The Netherlands exempt certain postal, telegraphic and telephone services. As these are provided by Government enterprises it is felt simpler administratively to fix a price for the service which would include any tax that might be charged. It is accepted that this extra charge cannot be credited by business enterprises. Most other countries appear to levy full taxes on these services.

Group 4 Betting, Gaming and Lotteries
Betting transactions will logically enough be exempt from VAT. However, a charge for admission to any premises or the granting of a right to take part in a game or the provision of facilities by a club to its members will not be exempt and will be subject to VAT, in the same way as any other entertainment or catering services. It is only the actual money wagered which will be exempt. Certain types of betting are already caught by specific taxes.

A typical gambler might stake £1,000 in a year, but recover £900 in winnings. His expenditure is not £1,000 but £100. It would be unreasonable to impose VAT on the *turnover*: if this were attempted regular gamblers might seek to register as taxable persons so as to be able to credit the VAT content on their winnings! (This also accounts for the alarming figures often quoted for national "expenditure" on gambling: the figure given is always of *turnover*: a fairer measure of *expenditure* would be the gross profit before costs, of bookmakers, pools promoters and others.)

There is a specific exemption in the Netherlands, where the general rule is that services are taxable unless excluded. In

Belgium and Sweden, services are only subject to VAT if specifically listed in the legislation. Gambling is not listed and therefore exempt. In Germany and France the position is a little ambiguous. Germany excludes from VAT forms of gambling where the gambler cannot influence the result. France only taxes "affaires" or businesses which apparently excludes gambling.

Group 5 Finance

This group exempts transactions concerned with the transfer of money, the granting of credit and dealings in securities. Obviously, transactions in money should not be subject to the same type and rates of tax as transactions in goods and services. The implications of this exemption are, although inevitable, far reaching and are discussed in Chapter 16.

Group 6 Education

This exempts any charge for the provision of education by a school or university or other education of the same type which is provided otherwise than for profits. The definition includes training in any form of art. It does appear at first sight as if the commercial provision of instructional training, such as by correspondence colleges, may be taxable. The exemption extends to the supply of any goods or services or the provision of any instruction supplemental to the provision of eligible education. This Group also exempts the provision by a youth club of facilities available to its members.

France also appears to grant similar exemptions including them in the categories of "public interest" or "social or cultural significance". Germany specifically exempts services rendered by schools. The Netherlands law has provisions enabling the Government to exempt specifically certain educational services with a general requirement that they should be provided by non-profit organisations. The exemption extends to lectures subject to the approval of the Minister of Finance provided that the fees are intended mainly to cover expenses, and also to youth work services rendered by organisations approved by the Government.

Group 7 Health

Most types of medical services are exempt. However, the inputs to such services will in general be taxable but drugs will normally be covered by the zero rating afforded to pharmaceutical products if they are supplied on prescription. The exemption extends to goods or services provided by registered opticians and dental technicians and any goods supplied in connection with the provision of medical or surgical treatment. (It appears that surgical equipment and other goods supplied *to* exempt suppliers will be subject to VAT which will, of course, not be recoverable. The implications of this should be further examined, as they doubtless will be by the trade associations concerned).

France generally applies the intermediate rate to medical services but hospitals operated by a local authority are exempt. Belgium certainly exempts medical services as it appears do most other countries.

Group 8 Burial and Cremation

These are exempt. There is a similar exemption in the Netherlands. Belgium and France impose reduced rates.

14. Exemptions and Zero Rating – Other Countries

In this Chapter we examine a number of categories of goods and services which are afforded special treatment in other countries but which are subject to tax at the standard rate in the United Kingdom. Traders in these categories will, with or without adequate justification, be likely to be pressing for special treatment.

Sales by Artists of Their Own Work

These are exempted in Denmark and Sweden but there is no provision in the United Kingdom. This is a difficult one. It would seem consistent on cultural grounds to exempt or zero rate works of art in the same way as books. On the other hand there is a difficulty of defining the border line of a work of art and a piece of furniture.

Artists with sales of under £5000 per annum need not register and will therefore be exempt. They will not be able to recover the tax element in paints and canvasses, but their private customers will not have to pay VAT on the element in price representing the work "value added" of the artist himself. Of course, if the artist sells to a gallery, which presumably will have a turnover in excess of £5000 per annum, the customer will pay VAT. In such a case it might pay the artist to register as a taxable person even if he is below the £5000 limit to avoid the "sandwich effect" on the VAT content of his own purchases. Artists working on commissions may find they can keep their turnover below £5000 by having clients supply canvas and paints. They would charge only for the work. Cf the "plumber" example in Chapter 2.

Services Rendered by Lawyers and Other Professional Men

These are exempt in Belgium and France. They are not to be exempted or zero rated in the United Kingdom. This has caused some comment. Businesses are not affected. The fact that there is a 10% VAT added on to professional bills does not concern them as they can claim a credit. Services rendered to non-resident clients will be zero rated in the normal way. It is only private individuals who will effectively bear the tax.

The most important use of lawyers' services by private citizens is probably in connection with house purchase. As explained in Chapter 18 the construction and transfer of new houses is zero rated and it may be that if the *seller* pays the lawyer's bill the VAT content will be recoverable. Doubtless attempts will be made to achieve this happy result. We shall have to wait and see whether the Customs and Excise regard this as a reasonable result to whether they will issue Regulations under their powers to disallow the credit of the input tax.

Theatres, Orchestras and Museums

Germany exempts these when they are owned by central or local Government authorities. The Netherlands also exempts cultural services provided that these are rendered on a non-profit basis and also provided that they are not unfairly competing with profitable enterprises. An art gallery might be exempt but a municipal theatre which was competing with a commercial theatre might on this principle be denied the exemption.

Travellers' Luggage etc.

Denmark specifically exempts the importation of goods not subject to customs duties such as travellers' luggage, sports prizes and certain articles imported by persons enjoying diplomatic or consular privileges. It is presumably not the intention of the United Kingdom to tax these but it is probably considered that they are automatically exempted as non-commercial transactions on the general rule. They are exempt in practice in other EEC countries.

15. Other Revenue Duties

In general VAT is intended to replace purchase tax and SET. It is a broadly based low rate tax on some goods and services which previously escaped purchase tax and now have to bear their share of the burden, but the effective rate of tax on goods suffering the higher rates of purchase tax will be reduced. This does *not* apply to certain revenue duties notably those on alcohol, tobacco, matches, mechanical lighters, petrol, and other hydrocarbon oils. These will continue to suffer the higher rates of tax plus (except in the case of hydrocarbon oils which are zero rated) VAT as well.

There will continue to be excise duty on alcoholic drinks, tobacco, matches, mechanical lighters and hydrocarbon oils. All of these, except hydrocarbon oils, will also be included within the scope of VAT. VAT will eventually be collected on the final retail price including excise duty. Unless excise duties were correspondingly reduced, there would be an increase in the total tax burden on these commodities. It is probable that the duties will be reduced but this will depend on the economic situation at the time of the 1973 Budget. As the excise duties are specific (e.g. on alcohol or tobacco content) rather than on final selling price any adjustment can only be approximate. This point is discussed in more detail in Chapter 12. Hydrocarbon oils are to be exempt so there will be no question of adjusting the rate.

If the rates of excise duties are reduced, this will produce a problem for those already holding tax-paid stock. This is the same problem as in the case of purchase tax paid stocks; the same solutions, discussed in Chapter 8, are appropriate.

The Car Tax

For Revenue reasons motor cars are to be added to the category of goods suffering an extra element of tax. In addition to VAT there will be a special "car tax" at 10% on the *wholesale* value of new and imported motor cars (Clause 51). The rate of purchase tax on cars was reduced in the 1972 Budget to 25% of the wholesale price and the net effect will be a further slight reduction in the total tax burden as from 1st April, 1973. The exact comparison depends on the size of the retail mark-up. The special tax, like purchase tax, is levied on the wholesale value while VAT falls on the retail value. If a car sells for £800 wholesale £1,000 retail, both tax exclusive, the present level of purchase tax would be £200 making the retail price £1,200. For the VAT the wholesaler has to collect £80 special tax plus £80 VAT. The price to the retailer £960. The retailer would have to charge the customer £1,080 plus £108 VAT but will be able to credit the £80 VAT input tax against the amount due to the Customs & Excise. He would collect £1,188 from the customer and pay £960 to the wholesaler plus £28 net VAT to the Customs & Excise. This leaves him with his clear margin of £200 as before. The total tax is £80 special tax plus £108 VAT making £188 in all, slightly less than the present purchase tax. The effect of the procedure is that VAT is levied on the special tax making the latter effectively 11%, not 10% of the wholesale value.

16. Financial Services, Insurance and Terminal Markets

VAT is a tax on the delivery to ultimate consumers of goods and services. It would be inappropriate to apply this principle to transactions involving flows of money. Banks and insurance companies do provide a service but the true economic value of the actual services they render is only a tiny fraction of the substantial sums of money handled.

In the course of a three month period an individual might pass £2,000 through his bank account and the bank might charge £5 for the operation of the account. If VAT is to be levied at all it would have to be on the £5 rather than on the £2,000. In principle there is no reason why VAT should not apply provided that it is appreciated the sum of £2,000 has no relationship whatsoever to the value of the services rendered. Banks in fact make most of their profit not from bank charges but from the difference between the borrowing and the lending rate. It would in principle be possible to impose VAT on interest payments and receipts but this would be very complicated and would distort the structure of money market. Banks tend on balance to borrow money from individuals and lend it to traders. Traders would not particularly mind paying VAT on their overdraft interest as they would get a credit but it would be a substantial extra burden on individuals. The difficulty in defining what constitutes an export transaction might well be insuperable. All countries have found it much more practicable simply to exempt interest from VAT and this precedent is to be followed in the United Kingdom. If interest is to be exempted so must the charge on accounts and on money transmission services. In the above example of the individual who passes £2,000 through his account, the bank might well have waived its charges if he had typically kept £500 as a working balance on current account. A bank can either pay a full competitive rate for the use of the money entrusted to it and then charge a full price for the services it renders; or it can render services free or at an undercharge because it has (or hopes to have) the use of money at a nil or very low interest cost.

Similarly with insurance the absolute sums of money changing hands are far larger than the value of the services rendered. Assume 10,000 people insure their car with a particular insurance company. Collectively they expect to suffer £200,000 worth of damage or third party claims in the course of the year. If they did not insure, most of them would lose nothing, many more would suffer a loss that they could afford; but the unlucky few would incur losses of £1,000, £5,000 or more. The object of insurance is to spread the risk. If the insurance company charges a premium of £25 it would have a premium income of £250,000 against claims for £200,000. It is performing the "service" of enabling the motorist to spread risks and incurs administrative costs in providing this service. The cost to the motorist of this *service* is £50,000 and not £250,000. With life assurance the margins are even finer and the greater part of the total premiums paid are in fact invested on behalf of the policy holders and subsequently returned to them with the benefit of interest and capital appreciation on the underlying investments.

Rather than undertaking the virtually impossible task of defining what is the real value of the "service" rendered by financial intermediaries the United Kingdom like other countries is simply providing that the services of insurance companies and insurance brokers shall be exempt. Also exempted are transactions involved with the payment and transmission of money and making advance of any credit and any commissions earned in connection with these services. It appears that VAT *will* be due on stockbrokers' *commissions* although not on the principal amount nor on jobbers' or other share dealers' profits. This still needs clarification.

Note that the transactions are *exempted* rather than zero rated which means that bank and insurance companies cannot in respect of their exempt business make a reclaim for the input taxes. On balance this probably gives approximately the right answer. On strict logic the services element in these transactions would be taxed but there are practical difficulties determining what part of the transaction really represents the cost of services. Looking at it the other way around, the market value of the services is equal to the costs incurred by the bank, or insurance company, in rendering the exempt services plus the profit. The costs consist in part of value-added taxed inputs and in part of non-taxed expenditure, mainly wages and salaries. Private customers only bear VAT indirectly on the taxed inputs which is less than the tax they would pay on strict logical basis. On the other hand taxable traders, because of the sandwich effect, are slightly worse off than they would be if VAT could be applied consistently to banking and insurance services. As this sandwich tax is passed forward to the consumer, overall the consumer is a little undertaxed on his direct financial and insurance transactions, but a little overtaxed to the extent to which these services are rendered to traders in connection with other goods and services he ultimately buys.

Banks, particularly merchant banks, will find themselves rendering both exempt and taxable services. Fees charged for portfolio management appear to be taxable. Fees for arranging a loan would be exempt but fees for negotiating an acquisition or merger or for advising a company which is subject to a take-over bid appear to be taxable. On the wording of the draft Bill it seems as though a fee for arranging an issue of fixed interest stocks might be exempt while a fee for arranging a new issue of equity would not be. Both will need clarification.

Where financial and insurance services are rendered to non-residents there are provisions in which the Treasury can by Order permit traders to treat these as zero rated rather than exempt.

Merchant banks will therefore have to divide their activities into those which are taxable or zero rated, and those which are exempt, and the cost of inputs would have to be allocated between these transactions in the manner discussed in Chapter 9. As explained in Chapter 2 it will not now be necessary to reorganise the corporate structure but will be possible to divide the whole group of companies into two or more "taxable persons" with a sub-division that could cut across normal corporate structure.

Terminal Markets

It is recognised that commodity markets will require special treatment. There are in London very important futures markets in metals, grains, fibres, vegetable oils, cocoa, coffee, rubber and sugar. It is possible in such markets to buy or sell these commodities at a price fixed on the day of the trade but for delivery at such future date which may be a year or more ahead. Quite often the buyer or seller, or both, will be non-resident in the UK. Sometimes, but very rarely, the futures contract will be settled by the buyer actually taking delivery from and paying the seller for the commodity in question. Usually the transaction is simply reversed. The purchase might be of sugar for October 1972 delivery and the price of £70 per ton fixed perhaps on a day in February. Sometime before October the trader will close his transaction by selling a similar quantity also for October delivery. If he sells at £80 per ton he will make a profit and will be paid the sum of £10 times the number of tons involved less commission. If the price is £60 he makes a loss.

The purchaser of the futures contract might be a manufacturer who knows he needs sugar in October and wants to protect himself against a rise in price before that date. Even so, he would not normally take delivery on his contract. When he needed the sugar he would simply buy it through trade channels at current market prices and at the same time reverse his futures contract. If the price had indeed risen by that date he would have to pay more for his actual sugar but he would be compensated by the profit on his futures contract. Similarly if the price had fallen he would get his actual sugar much cheaper but would in effect be paying the price at which he hedged because of the off-setting loss on his contract. The seller of the futures contract may have been a sugar producer who wanted to ensure the price of his new crop in advance. He too would normally reverse his futures contract, selling the actuals to trade channels.

Where a UK trader purchases and takes delivery of a commodity he will have to pay VAT in accordance with the normal rules. It would be unreasonable to impose VAT on futures contracts which are subsequently reversed. The sensible rule therefore would be that VAT would become payable only on the occasion of actual delivery. Even then it is arguable that VAT should be on current market prices rather than on the contract price. If it were not so traders who had hedged and seen the price rise would take actual delivery on the contract and only pay VAT on their hedge price while if the price had in fact fallen they would reverse their contract and buy at a new low price. Normally this would not be a worthwhile exercise as most importers of taxable commodities would be able to obtain a credit for the input tax at whatever level it was imposed.

The only other question is whether the commission charged by the commodity broker should be subject to VAT or whether it should be exempt. If it is exempt should zero rating privileges be given where the service is rendered to a non-resident trader?

All that Clause 26 says, stripped of legal language, is that the Customs and Excise recognise that there are problems, that they intend to find a solution, and that the solutions might be different for different markets.

17. Agriculture and Fisheries

Most farm products will be zero rated in accordance with the definition given in Group 1 of Schedule 4 to the Finance Bill. Although farmers will not have to charge VAT on the products, they will have to register and indeed it will be substantially to their advantage for them to register. They should certainly consider registration even if their sales are likely to be below £5,000. They will be able to reclaim from the Customs and Excise any VAT charged on goods and services bought by them in the course of their trade as farmers.

Group 1 includes not only "food of a kind used for human consumption" but also animal feeding stuffs and seeds for growing human or animal foods. The Group also includes live animals of a kind generally used as or yielding or producing food for human consumption and "animal" is defined to include birds, fishes and shell-fish. It appears that horses and pheasants will be taxable but cows and ducks will be zero-rated. There are a number of categories of food and drink which are not zero rated but these are all manufactured or packaged, foods which will not normally concern the farmer or market gardener.

Farmers will have to charge and account for VAT on sales of second-hand machinery and (apparently) on the sale of timber. Certain transactions between farmers might be subject to VAT. Examples will be the hiring out of machinery or the undertaking of repairs for neighbours by a farmer who has workshop facilities. This has only administrative significance as the farmer making the payment will be able to recover the tax as described below. In these cases it might be sensible for the Customs and Excise to agree to waive tax on these inter-farmer transactions subject to administrative safeguards.

The farmer will have to register in the normal way but he will actually have to charge VAT on few, if any, of his sales. As most of his sales are zero rated goods his VAT "output tax" will be nil or at least very small. At the end of each accounting period he will have to make a return to the Customs and Excise in the same way as any other trader showing his output tax, even if it is nil, and claiming relief for input tax. He must keep all invoices from suppliers which include VAT. The total of the VAT shown on all these invoices is his "input tax". Generally his input tax will exceed his output tax. He will be able to reclaim from the Customs and Excise the whole of the input tax less any output tax he has charged his own customers.

Only a small proportion of a farmer's expenditure will represent taxed inputs. A large part of his expenses will be wages and rent which do not come into the VAT calculation. Purchases of animal feeding stuffs, feeds, plants and animals and fuel are zero rated as described above. (It is not clear from the text of the Bill that hatching eggs are zero rated but presumably they will be.) The main items concerned will probably be machinery, ironmongery, sacks and machinery repairs. Veterinary Surgeons' bills and animal medicines will also be subject to VAT and the input tax will have to be recovered or credited. There are also less obvious items such as Solicitors' and Accountants' fees and stationery. Many farmers probably buy their stationery and account books over the counter for cash. They should make a point of obtaining a tax invoice so they can get a reclaim on the 10% VAT charge.

Rent is in general *exempt*. A farmer who lets off some of his fields or who lets grazing rights is carrying on a partially exempt business and could in principle be denied the right to make reclaims of input tax on those parts of his business connected with the letting of land. This could create the problem we discussed in Chapter 9. In practice farmers will probably be able to argue that none of their purchases are directly connected with the earning of income from letting. Clause 3 permits the Customs to waive their right to an adjustment where exempt trade is negligible: this is a suitable case.

Certain types of "letting" are not covered by the exemption and *are* subject to VAT. Some of these will concern farmers. Any charges made for the provision of camping or caravan sites and any charges made for shooting or fishing rights are subject to VAT. The farmer must add VAT to his charges and must, if called upon to do so, issue a tax invoice. He must account for the tax he has collected to the Customs and Excise in the normal way but unless these activities are a very substantial part of his business, the chances are that he will still have a net reclaim at the end of the accounting period.

Normally, VAT accounting periods are for three months but traders can elect for a monthly accounting period if this would suit them better. The conditions for the election have not yet been set out. Because most of their outputs are zero rated farmers will normally have a refund at the end of each accounting period. It could suit them better to have a monthly accounting period, and to obtain prompt repayment. With quarterly repayments, refund of VAT for purchases made in January, February and March (assuming the farmer was on that particularly monthly cycle) would be made on or around 30th April. If he elected for monthly accounting, he could obtain a refund on his January purchases at the end of February (two months earlier), on his February purchases at the end of March (one month earlier). If his taxable purchases were £1,000 each month with a £100 VAT element, the effect of the election would be that for four months in the year he would be £200 in pocket, in another four months in the year he would be £100 in pocket. If he is paying bank overdraft interest at 10% per annum the overall annual saving works out at just £10. What he then has to decide is whether the extra work of making monthly reclaims more than outweighs this interest saving.

Fish are also zero rated. Fishermen therefore are in much the same position as farmers. They will have to register but will normally make a net reclaim from the Customs & Excise at the end of each accounting period.

As explained in Chapter 6 "Self supply" is a taxable

transaction. Fortunately this will not concern most farmers and market gardeners as their own principal self supply (food) is zero rated anyway. The Inspector of Taxes will continue to be interested in assessing how much of their own produce they consume. The Customs and Excise will not.

18. Building and Land

Group 7 of Schedule 4 *zero rates* the construction of buildings whilst Group 1 of Schedule 5 *exempts* certain transactions in land. These provisions have to be looked at together. Their combined effect is that no VAT will be charged on normal transactions in property. House purchasers will have to pay VAT on their surveyor's, solicitor's and estate agent's charges. Unless there are special provisions in the Regulations it will therefore seem advantageous to ensure that where a house is sold by a builder he should pay all these fees (on which he would get a recovery on input tax) and recover them from the other party by an increase in the price. Where the transaction is between a buyer and a seller neither of whom is a taxable person (e.g. the sale of an owner-occupied house to a new owner-occupier) there does not appear to be scope for interposing a taxable person as an intermediary between them. The resale would be exempt and recovery of input tax would be denied.

Reading the two provisions together one finds that there are a number of exceptions. For instance, excluded from the exceptions are the provisions of accommodation in hotels and boarding houses or in houses, flats or caravans used for holiday accommodation. Short-term accommodation in other words will be subject to VAT at the normal rate. Also subject to VAT will be the granting of camping facilities, car parking charges and charges made for shooting or fishing rights. Looking at Schedule 4 Group 7 we also find that repair and maintenance work and the services of an architect, surveyor or consultant are subject to VAT at the normal rate. If these services were rendered to a builder whose outputs were zero rated, the tax would be recoverable in the normal way.

The zero rating provision of Schedule 4 Group 7 covers "the granting by a person constructing a building of a major interest in or in any part of the building or its site". A major interest is defined to cover a freehold or a lease for a period exceeding 21 years. It is not clear from the Bill what precisely is meant by a 21 year lease in this case. Presumably rent revision clauses at 7 and 14 years would be in order but if either party had an option to break the lease within the period it would not. If break options were permitted, it would be possible so to word the rent revision provisions that one party or the other would be virtually certain to break, thus turning what was on paper a 21 year lease into what was, in practice, a shorter lease.

The exemption provision of Schedule 5 Group 1 includes "The grant, assignment or surrender of *any* interest in, or right over, land or of any licence to occupy land" subject to the exception noted above. This would cover rent or the grant of a shorter lease, but in this case the seller would be denied the right to recover any input tax. The intention of the zero rating provision is to allow recovery of input tax when the original builder puts up a building and sells it on a 21 year or longer lease. Subsequent transactions in the house would simply be exempted.

Repair and maintenance are not zero rated and costs will be subject to VAT in the normal way. Group 7, Item 3 zero rates the supply of materials and builders' hardware in connection with the construction, alteration or demolition of any building. This does *not* include any work, repair or maintenance and this may raise problems of definition. The purchase of goods for routine repairs will be subject to VAT in the normal way. The supply of goods for major alteration will be zero rated if alterations are carried out by direct labour. There is no provision for zero rating of builders' supplies for contractors putting up new buildings. They will be invoiced for the input tax in the normal way but will be able to recover it. The differential treatment for alterations is presumably intended to cover the likelihood of such work being done by direct labour.

The above provisions for construction and alteration

would also have the effect of zero rating the cost of the building put up by a business organisation for its own use by direct labour.

19. Antiques and Second Hand Goods

In general, second hand goods are subject to VAT in the normal way. Indeed, such a provision is necessary to give proper treatment to straightforward business transactions. If a business sells a second hand machine to another business, VAT will be charged but will be creditable as an input tax. A similar effect could be achieved by exempting such transactions, but this would raise difficulties with the definition of what was second hand and might open the way for avoidance manoeuvres.

It is different with transactions involving private individuals. An individual buys a new car for £1,100 including £100 of VAT. (There will also be the car tax which will have been collected at the wholesale level, but this is irrelevant to the present discussion as it only applies to newly manufactured or newly imported cars). Two years later he sells it to a dealer for £400. He is not a taxable person for VAT purposes so there is no VAT on this transaction. The dealer resells the car for £600. In the absence of special provisions he would have to charge £660 including £60 VAT notwithstanding the fact that the car had already paid VAT when it was first bought.

The position would be even worse with antiques. Someone buys a piece of furniture for £330 including £30 VAT. Some time later he sells it to a dealer for £600 but cannot recover the VAT he originally paid. The dealer resells for £900 to a private collector who must effectively pay £990, including £90 VAT. This collector sells to another dealer for £1,200, making a profit of only £210. (On £200 of this he must also pay capital gains tax). The third dealer sells to the third collector for £1,650, including £150 of VAT. Note that in no case can the dealer recover an input tax as the property is changing hands from a taxable person (a dealer) to a non-taxable person (a private individual collector). This would be the "sandwich effect" with a vengeance. In the example told VAT would be £270 on a final net sale price of £1,500.

It will also be seen that quite apart from dealer's margins (not notoriously small in the antique business) there is a substantial additional incentive for private collectors to seek out each other and to avoid VAT by cutting out the dealers altogether. It will also be seen that the export customers can buy from a dealer at a much lower price than the price at which a domestic buyer has to pay although both of them get the same price back on resale. Collectors of expensive items sometimes regard themselves as investors. Rightly or wrongly they hope to make a profit. Even those who are buying mainly for aesthetic satisfaction can only afford to pay the prices that they do because they recognise that they have a durable asset on which they could recover some at least of the purchase price if necessary. Realists know that if they have to sell and if there had been no change in the general level of market prices, they might lose (say) 30% of their outlay. For the foreign buyer this will continue to be true. With unmitigated VAT, the fall would be not from £1,000 to £700, but from £1,100 to £700, or 36.67%. This is a material difference.

What is, in fact, proposed is that there should be a compromise. Where second hand goods are bought from the public and are resold to the public the VAT element should only be on the dealer's own gross margin. This will still distort the market as between individual to individual sales and as between domestic and foreign buyers. It might give an advantage to the smaller dealer who can claim exemption as a small trader on the grounds that his sales are less than £5,000 per annum. It is not clear what this definition will mean in practice in this case. If a dealer buys goods from the public for £8,000 and resells them for £12,000, he will have to account for VAT only on the profit of £4,000. As his taxable outputs are only £4,000 he could, on one definition, claim the small trader exemption. On the other hand, his absolute sales are £12,000 which may take him outside the definition. In the latter case, he might be able to come within the exemption by changing his methods of business. Instead of buying for his own account he might take goods into stock as the agent for the vendor without taking legal title to them. He would then resell on "commission", and it would be this commission (in the example, £4,000) which would be his turnover in this case. He might not like this if it involved disclosing his mark-up but it might be possible to avoid this by a suitable form of contract with the vendor. He might, for instance, give the vendor an "advance" against the security of the goods in stock and have a form of contract by which he had the right for a period of twelve months to sell as agent collecting the whole of the surplus as his commission. At the end of the year the goods would become his property.

Auctioneers who do so on commission will charge VAT on such commission. In the United Kingdom fine art auctioneers collect their commission from the vendor. If the bidder bids £100 the auctioneer retains £10 of this (assuming a 10% commission rate), and hands over £90 to the vendor. If VAT is charged and the auctioneer does not absorb this into his commission structure, the vendor would have to pay £10 plus £1 VAT and collect only £89. If he were a trader this would be a tax input and would not, as such, concern him. If he were a non-resident no commission would be due as the transaction would (apparently) be zero rated as an export of services.

In some other countries, the custom is different. The purchaser pays the commission and if he bids £100 he would have to pay £110 including a 10% commission. (In fact, on this basis, a commission rate of 11.1% would have to be charged if it were to be exactly equivalent to the UK system of 10% commission rate). VAT has to be added on in addition. In fact, there are generally also auction and transfer taxes in other countries — one of the reasons for the supremacy of the London fine art market.

In any situation where an agent mediates between buyer and seller taking a commission from one side or the other, it will be desirable under VAT to ensure that as far as possible the agent acts for and claims his commission from either the non-resident party if there is one or from a trader who can obtain a credit for the input tax. He should avoid charging the commission to a resident individual non-trader but will obviously have to do so if both buyer and seller have this status. It will not, in practice, be possible to treat each case on its merits especially as the identity of the seller is not usually disclosed and identity of the buyer is not known until after the sale is over. The appropriate top bidder is different under the two systems. What may happen is that sales are divided into two parts, the vendors having the option to put their goods into whichever part suits them. In part 1 commission would be for the account of the vendor. Professional dealers and non-residents would sell their goods in this part. In part 2 commission would be paid by the purchaser. Resident private individuals would place goods into this part, and there would be a saving of VAT at least in the cases where the purchaser was a non-resident or a dealer. Private individual purchasers could offer a slightly keener price (by 1%) if they wished to bid for items in part 1.

There is a strong case on general grounds for exempting works of art and second hand goods generally. The difficulty is one of definition. For instance, with second hand goods, exemption might be limited to goods of more than a certain number of years old. A less rigorous test might be effected if it could be established that the original purchaser had paid VAT or purchase tax on them. Exemption rather than zero rating seems appropriate except for the administrative problems this might cause to those handling both new and antique goods.

There is also a case, as discussed elsewhere, for exempting or zero rating artists on the sale of their own works but here again the difficulty is defining a work of art in such a way as to exclude decorative or even useful household objects. It is one thing to know a work of art when you see one but quite another to define it in a legal and unambiguous way for this purpose.

20. Exports

Exports are zero rated. As explained in Chapter 3 this means that not only is there no tax on the export transaction itself, but the exporter can obtain a refund of any input tax borne at previous stages. This is not an export subsidy, it is simply cancelling out and refunding tax which has already been collected. Export customers do not at present pay purchase tax or indeed, any other UK Customs and Excise duties. There is a slight improvement in the new arrangements. Previously, goods exported may have had as an element in their cost of production some component of SET and possibly a little purchase tax, on goods bought by businesses. To the extent to which these are replaced by a recoverable VAT there will be a small competitive advantage.

Take the simple case of a pure export merchant who buys goods from UK manufacturers for re-sale to export customers. His purchases exclusive of tax in an accounting period are £200,000. He takes a 7½% margin and resells for £215,000. In fact, his supplier will invoice him for £220,000 including £20,000 of VAT. If both transactions were settled immediately the trader would be £5,000 out of pocket but would have a claim of £20,000 recoverable input tax from Customs and Excise. When he received this he would have his gross profit of £15,000. In practice the transactions will be for credit rather than for cash. Export merchants will certainly take advantage of the option for a one month accounting period and would therefore receive the repayment from the Customs and Excise one month after the end of the month in which the supplier's invoice was received. On average this is just over six weeks after the invoice. If the export merchant both gives and receives three months credit he will normally expect to get a repayment from the Customs and Excise (which in this case is rather more than his own profit margin) before his customer pays him and before he has to pay his suppliers. If the supplier requires payment by the export merchant earlier than the last day of the month following the month in which the goods were invoiced the effect of VAT will be slightly to squeeze the export merchant's liquidity. If he obtains longer payment terms the effect of VAT will be to improve his liquidity. For this purpose the payment terms granted by the export merchant himself to his overseas customer are (although relevant to his own cash requirements) not important in deciding whether or not the introduction of VAT will worsen or improve the relative liquidity position.

All countries zero rate exports and indeed this is required by the EEC Directive. VAT is intended to fall on the ultimate consumer and to be collected by his own country of residence regardless of the origin of the goods. The definition of what constitutes an export is not quite consistent from country to country. The United Kingdom legislation goes as far as possible towards being all-inclusive.

The general provision is Clause 12 (6) "a supply of goods is zero rated. . . . .if the Commissioners are satisfied that the persons buying the goods

    a. has exported them, or
    b. has shipped them for use as stores on a voyage or flight to an eventual destination outside the United Kingdom or as merchandise for sale by retail to persons carried on such voyage or flight in a ship or aircraft".

There are provisions dealing with cases where the Commissioners "are satisfied that the goods have been *or are to be* exported". This will probably include the transfer of goods to bonded warehouses. This provision would also enable the Customs and Excise to treat bona fide export merchants as if they were themselves export customers. In the example above the supply *to* the export merchant would be zero rated. The merchant would simply pay £200,000 without the necessity of having to make a reclaim. Any such provision would have to be discretionary to prevent possible abuses. Penalties can be imposed under Clause 12 (8) if goods claimed to have been exported are in fact found to be in the United Kingdom or if other conditions imposed by the Customs and Excise are not fulfilled. The penalty is the forfeiture of the goods and the payment of the tax.

The term "exported" is not defined but in the case of goods the term seems clear enough and will normally mean delivery outside the United Kingdom. Delivery to a ship or aircraft as stores or for sales to passengers is also specifically included as if it were an export provided that the ultimate destination of a ship or aircraft is outside the United Kingdom. In the case of foreign visitors no doubt the present purchase tax rules will continue to apply, and there will be limited arrangements for actually taking delivery of VAT free goods in the UK and declaring them to Customs at the port of exit.

Where goods are sent by a company or firm to its overseas branch there is no change of legal ownership and in the Netherlands it would be argued that there was no taxable event. This does not matter in practice. The purchase price is creditable in the normal way. It does not matter that there is no *taxable* sale because of an export or because the goods have been absorbed into stock. In the United Kingdom such transactions will probably be treated as an export. Although the overseas branch has no separate legal existence it will appear to be excluded from the definition of "taxable person" and *would* therefore be a transaction. This point is really a lawyer's quibble of no practical significance.

The real difficulties of the definition of export come in connection with the export of services. These are discussed in Chapter 22.

21. Imports

As I have explained, all countries zero rate exports. When goods cross frontiers the exporting country refunds all the VAT it has so far collected. Correspondingly, the importing country must collect VAT at the appropriate rate on the full value of the import. Clause 1 (1) of the Bill imposes VAT on the supply of goods and "on the importation of goods into the United Kingdom". This is simple enough and perfectly logical but involves one or two practical complications.

First of all, this is an exceptional case where VAT might have to be paid by someone who is *not* a trader or "taxable person". This would happen if someone ordered goods by post from abroad for personal use or brought them back in person from an overseas trip. It is provided in Clause 11 of the Bill that the valuation is the value for Customs purposes plus the amount of Customs duty payable. Administratively, VAT will be collected in cases at the same time as and in connection with Customs duties. There will be no difference in procedure from that now applied on purchase tax. The limited concessions for returning travellers will continue to apply. At present when dutiable goods are declared in excess of the concessions both Customs duty and purchase tax (the latter often is just a rule of thumb estimate) are applied.

Where the importer is a trader a somewhat simpler procedure is available. Consider the case of a pure import merchant who imports goods from abroad and resells them more or less immediately to his own customers. He buys goods to the value of £100,000 including Customs duties. If the strict procedure was observed he would have at the same time to pay £10,000 VAT. This would be required from him at the time of clearing customs. He would then be in the position of having purchases of £100,000 and an input tax credit of £10,000. He sells the goods for £108,000 adding £10,800 VAT on to his invoice. His customer would in due course pay to him £118,800. One month after the end of the accounting period he would have to pay over £10,800 less £10,000 of creditable input tax. This creditable tax is of course the VAT he paid over himself to the Customs and Excise. He would be out of pocket for the £10,000 until he either received payment from his own customer or reclaimed it as a credit from the Customs and Excise.

Clause 18 provides that Customs and Excise may permit the importer to clear Customs *without* paying VAT "subject to such conditions or restrictions as the Commissioners may impose for the protection of the revenue". As the VAT on import is simultaneously treated as a creditable input tax the two cancel out. The import merchant or indeed any trader simply pays out the full amount of VAT, in this case £10,800 on the resale by him of the goods imported. This is a considerable simplification and greatly helps the cash flow of traders. Similar provisions have been developed in most other countries.

This procedure will presumably not be available to a foreign exporter who transfers goods into the United Kingdom as his own property but for eventual resale. Unless the exporting company or firm has registered in the United Kingdom as a "taxable person" VAT will be payable on clearing Customs. In practice it will probably suit such foreign exporters to register.

The legislation provides that where particular goods or services would be exempted or zero rated if supplied in the United Kingdom the corresponding treatment is given for imports. Clause 16 gives enabling powers for giving relief on goods imported. This provision will presumably be used in cases where administrative convenience outweighs the likely revenue.

The Channel Islands and the Isle of Man
The Treaty of Accession to the European Economic Community specifically provides that there is no obligation on the

Channel Islands and the Isle of Man to harmonise their tax systems although they will form part of the Customs Union. After the transitional period therefore, there will be no Customs duties on goods entering the United Kingdom from these territories. However, in principle, imports from them will be subject to VAT in the normal way, while exports to them will be zero rated.

The Isle of Man is considering introducing VAT. If this is in fact done Clause 49 of the Bill provides in effect that arrangement can be made for treating the Isle of Man as if it were part of the United Kingdom for the purpose of VAT. Taxable persons in the United Kingdom will be treated as taxable persons in the Isle of Man and vice versa. An export to the Isle of Man would not be zero rated but would bear VAT under the normal rules. If the purchaser was an Isle of Man trader he would be entitled to credit any tax against his own liability. Where goods are imported from the Isle of Man VAT would have been charged and accounted for by the Isle of Man exporter. This would be allowed as a creditable tax input if the importer was a UK trader. There are enabling provisions by which arrangements could be made for sharing revenue between the two jurisdictions.

None of the Channel Islands has any present intention of introducing VAT. If at a later stage they were to do so, no doubt the same arrangements could be made.

22. Exports and Imports of Services and Intangible Transactions

(This chapter is somewhat technical and could be omitted on a first reading).

International transactions in goods involve no serious problems of definition. If the goods leave the country they are exported; if they enter the country they are imported. There is movement of tangible items, and the only question is at what moment of time the transaction is deemed to take place. With services it is more difficult and there is no clear principle that can be applied consistently. Article 6 (3) of the EEC Second Directive states "the place of a rendering of services is deemed to be located, in principle, at the place where the service rendered, the right transferred or granted, or the object rented is used or exploited". Different countries have interpreted this in different ways. Applying this in one way, we could say that if the service is rendered in the United Kingdom it is not an "export" but is taxable. On this basis if a foreign customer were to ask a United Kingdom firm of engineering consultants to design them a power station the service would arguably be rendered in the United Kingdom and the fee would *not* be zero rated. As the foreign customer would not usually be a taxable person within the United Kingdom he might not be able to obtain a credit. If his own country imposed a VAT it would not (under any present laws) give him a credit for the foreign VAT.

Then again, the question of tax liability might depend on where plans were handed over. Similarly, if a foreign businessman consults an English lawyer in England he might bear tax while if the meeting took place abroad he would enjoy zero rating. Patent licences can produce even odder results as discussed below. Clearly these are both unsatisfactory bases. It is in principle adopted in Germany but with extensive reliefs, intended, not always successfully, to cover the type of case just mentioned.

The other principle would be to say that the supply of a service is zero rated if the customer is not a resident of the United Kingdom. Very broadly this is the approach we are to apply but this too can produce odd results if consistently applied. For instance a barber cutting the hair of an American visitor would not on the strict principle have to charge VAT. This might be acceptable although complicated. How would the visitor establish his status? A hair-cut is at least personal but it would not be so easy to make sure that a foreign visitor was not using his tax exemption to have the laundry done free of tax for his hosts and their sisters and their cousins and their aunts. Clearly therefore it is not practicable to zero rate otherwise taxable services rendered to individuals actually within the United Kingdom.

Where exempt services are rendered to non-residents there is the question of whether the exempt trader can claim zero rating in respect of services rendered to a foreign customer. He would then be able to recover his input tax. A common situation concerns banking and insurance services which for practical reasons are exempt in most countries. There was a dispute in the Netherlands. A Dutch insurance company, as part of its business, insured foreign risks on behalf of foreign policyholders. The company claimed that, as exports, these should be zero rated and that it should be eligible to recover a proportion of its input taxes. The Dutch tax authorities argued that insurance was exempted and that even though the service was rendered to non-residents the company should *not* be allowed to recover any of its input taxes. Item 5 of Group 8 of Schedule 4 gives the United Kingdom Treasury power to make Orders permitting suppliers of banking and insurance services (normally exempted) to be zero rated. The intention is clearly to give the more favourable treatment but we shall have to wait for the actual Orders to see that the safeguards and administrative procedures are to be used.

Although there is no simple definition of the export of a

service, the list as given in Group 8 of Schedule 4 at least attempts to be as inclusive as possible. Briefly, these are treated as the export of services, services supplied by a UK agent to an overseas trader, the sale of advertising (or of services in connection with advertising) to an overseas trader and the supply to an overseas trader of any services not used in the United Kingdom unless these services are exempt. As explained above the Treasury may specifically permit the rendering of certain categories of insurance and financial services to be treated as a zero rated export even though they would, if rendered to a UK trader, be treated as exempted transactions.

Where services which are not exempt and which would be taxable in the normal way if rendered to a UK resident are rendered to an overseas *trader* they are zero rated provided that they are "services not used in the United Kingdom". However where services are rendered to an overseas *authority* the words in quotes are *omitted* from the text. It therefore appears that the rendering of services to an overseas *authority* are zero rated even when they are rendered *within* the United Kingdom. "Overseas authority" is defined as any State other than the United Kingdom or any part of or place within such a state. This appears to cover not only countries and sub-divisions of countries such as states, provinces or cantons but municipalities or local authorities down to the level of the equivalent of a parish council. It is provided that this treatment does *not* include the supply of any services to any agency or establishment of such a State or local authority within the United Kingdom. The supply of goods to an embassy is not of itself zero rated as an export although there might be diplomatic immunity. A public relations agency acting on behalf of a foreign government (or foreign holiday resort) could treat its services as zero rated, but if services were rendered to the resident representative of the foreign state, zero rating would not apply. The local representative could probably register as a "taxable person" and recover the input tax.

If an overseas trader sends goods to the United Kingdom for treatment or processing in such a way that the goods remain his own property and are subsequently exported, any charges made in the United Kingdom will be zero rated. This gives the same result as if the goods were imported and re-exported, the profit reflecting the fee that would otherwise be charged for the process.

In all the above the definition of "overseas trader" may be vital. He is defined as someone who carried on the business outside the United Kingdom and is neither resident nor (if a company) incorporated in the United Kingdom. This definition could create difficulties in practice. It would appear to exclude the rendering of services to a foreign unincorporated branch of a United Kingdom company or to a foreign unincorporated branch of a United Kingdom company or to a foreign company which happened to trade in the United Kingdom through an unincorporated branch. It would exclude the rendering of services to a trade carried on wholly outside the United Kingdom by a UK resident, to a partnership controlled outside the United Kingdom in which a UK resident is a partnership even though the income tax law affords such businesses the favourable treatment of Case V of Schedule D. It would also exclude the admittedly rare case of a company which happened to be incorporated in the United Kingdom but which was controlled and managed outside the United Kingdom and was treated as non-resident for all income tax and corporation tax purposes. Although in general the VAT law permits a domestic company or unincorporated business a flexible definition of "taxable person" without these definitions having to be followed by the corporate or tax structure the definition of an "overseas trader" is somewhat restrictive. It may be necessary to alter corporate forms or to create subsidiaries to insure that an overseas business actually falls within the definition.

There are obviously going to be loopholes by which services are rendered to an overseas trader as defined in a way that really benefits a United Kingdom trader. One possibility is already foreseen in the legislation. Advertising services are *not* to be zero rated where they are supplied to an overseas trader who is an agent or subsidiary of a United Kingdom business.

Licensing Transactions

Item 9 of Group 8 is "the granting, assignment or surrender of any right exercisable outside the United Kingdom". This would appear to include all kinds of royalties or lump sum payments received under licensing agreement for patents, copyrights, trademarks and know-how, provided that the licensee uses the rights outside the United Kingdom. Generally, in international licensing transactions, royalties *in* will be treated as exports of services while royalties *out* will be treated as payment for the import of services. Payments received from a non-resident in connection with the *United Kingdom* rights under a patent or copyright would *not* count as an export and would not be zero rated.

On the whole this seems to be the commonsense result. There could be one difficulty in practice. The UK company or individual might own a patent and license a foreign company for the world-wide rights including the United Kingdom. That element of the royalty reflecting the United Kingdom uses would not be zero rated and would suffer VAT. The licensee might have sub-licensed a UK manufacturer, or have in effect granted the rights to his UK subsidiary without payment. In either case the cost of the royalty would, directly or indirectly, enter into the cost of production of the final product. If, however, the licensee who actually paid the royalties is not himself a taxable person for VAT purposes within the United Kingdom there seems to be no procedure by which the VAT borne on the royalty payments could be allowed as credit. This situation could be avoided in one of two ways. Either the licensee could actually become a taxable person and pass the credit through or the obligation to pay the royalties could be assigned directly to the United Kingdom user.

There is a similar situation in the Netherlands where the zero rate applies only if the person to whom the service is rendered does not have the benefit of the service within the Netherlands. This is the case if the patent was enforceable only outside the Netherlands. Where the patent is applied within the Netherlands VAT does apply and it may be desirable to ensure there is a direct payment from a Netherlands trader without passing through a non-resident intermediary. The

Netherlands is, in fact, exceptional in having a procedure by which a non-resident trader can obtain a refund of any Dutch VAT charged to him and which he cannot credit against VAT due by him on Dutch output.

In Germany the general concept is that it is delivery which constitutes a taxable transaction and that it is the place of delivery rather than the residence of the customer which determines the VAT position. In the case of services this is the place where the activity is exclusively or mainly performed or where an action or situation is tolerated or an action is abstained from.

This definition can produce some odd results in the case of licensing transactions. Zero rating applies to royalties or lump sums received in Germany in consideration of the non-German rights under a patent. This has the same results as in the United Kingdom or the Netherlands but the answer is reached by what might seem to us to be a somewhat tortuous piece of legal reasoning. The main right conferred by a patent on its owner is the right to sue for infringement. A licence under a patent is therefore an agreement for consideration (the royalty) *not* to sue. The "services" which the licensor is rendering to the licensee is the service of abstaining from a law suit. If the rights in question are Canadian rights such a law suit would have to be in the Canadian courts. It therefore follows that the service of abstaining from instituting a law suit is rendered in Canada, and the transaction is zero rated in Germany.

This would be an irrelevant technicality — if it were not that the same type of reasoning produces the *wrong* answer in the case of know-how licences. A know-how licence involves unpatented technical information which may or may not be successfully kept secret. In the case of a patent the information is presumed to be available to anyone who cares to obtain a copy of the specification from the Patent Office. All that is needed is the right to use it. In the case of know-how it has to be imparted and it is the passing on the knowledge which is the "service" for VAT purposes. If German technicians visit the licencee's factory in another country and there impart their knowledge the service is rendered outside Germany and the payments will be zero rated. If, as so often happens, the know-how agreement provides for visits to the German licensor's factory and the training of the licencee's staff in Germany the service is rendered in Germany and VAT is chargeable. This could result in a "sandwich effect". This problem does actually arise in practice although the German tax authorities tend in the common case of mixed patent and know-how licences to permit the payment to be treated as mainly in connection with the patent.

There is a procedure in the Netherlands, but not apparently in Germany or the United Kingdom, by which a foreign trader who does not have a permanent establishment in the country and who has VAT charged to him (perhaps because of a technical deficiency in the legal definitions) can make an application to recover it. Such an overriding provision might be useful in dealing with the occasional hard cases that there must be in dealing with international trade in services.

It will be seen that VAT is due on the payment of a licence royalty to a foreign licensor. This is irrelevant, except from an administrative point of view, where the licensee is a UK taxable trader. It will be relatively rare for royalties to be paid by exempt traders except possibly in connection with education or health. Payment could be waived by Treasury Order under the provisions of Clause 16.

There is an interesting provision in France. "Inventors" do not have to pay VAT on receipts from the exploitation of their own inventions on the grounds that they are not traders but are carrying on a liberal profession. (There are also valuable income tax concessions). Where a foreign "inventor" receives royalties from a French source it is possible for there to be an exemption from VAT on the payment of a royalty which would otherwise be treated as an import of services. For this purpose a company can be treated as an inventor if the invention was made by its own dependent employees but not if it acquired the patent rights from a third party. There are provisions for giving effect to this in a number of double tax agreements including that with the United Kingdom. Where the granting of a licence is associated with the import of goods the exemption does not apply. This is intended to rule out the possibility of minimising liability to French VAT by associating imports at a low value with a payment for their right to use the import for particular process. At such a case the French tax authorities will adjust the value of the import to include that royalty payment. These provisions can apparently occasionally produce odd results. They are only relevant if the French licensee is not a taxable trader for VAT purposes but is either a consumer or an exempt trader.

In Belgium the supply of services includes the sale of a concession or monopoly for selling or purchasing; the sale of a concession, exclusive or otherwise, of the right to carry on a business or professional activity; the sale of a concession of patents, trademarks, author's rights, drawings, industrial models or similar rights. The words "or similar rights" include know-how transactions.

23. The Economics of VAT

This Chapter is not intended to be a rigorous treatment of the economics of taxation, a subject on which there is an extensive literature. It is rather intended to summarise some of the arguments for and against VAT, to explain the likely effects and to dispel a few misconceptions.

No one has yet devised a good tax. All taxes are unpopular, all can be shown to bear unduly harshly on some groups of individuals, most distort consumption patterns, and most, though not all, have disincentive side effects. All we can say is that some taxes are less bad than others.

Taxes are levied to pay for Government expenditure. This disadvantage of taxation must be balanced against the benefits derived from public services.

The art of taxation, therefore, is to finance a given level of government expenditure in the way that does least harm to other policy objectives, including the need to leave individuals with money in their pockets to spend exactly as they like. Taxation pays for politician-decided expenditure: what is left after taxation pays for individually-decided expenditure. We have to ask whether the government is giving us value for money. If certain government services were reduced or eliminated so that taxes could be reduced by £100 million would we, on balance, be better or worse off? It is not an easy question to answer. The various distorting effects of taxation become increasingly serious as the general burden of taxes rises. It is probably possible to collect 15% of the product of the country without many side effects, without having to worry unduly about the best form of taxation. Once the tax take rises much above 25% it becomes increasingly difficult to devise new taxes or to increase the rates of old ones without adverse consequences. At the same time rising government expenditure usually means tackling the less urgent and obvious problems, the familiar situation of diminishing returns. It is fairly safe to say that the first £1,000 million will probably be expenditure giving extremely good value for money and equally likely that the last £500 million is not. One of the problems is a Parliamentary procedure under which proposals for government good works are discussed, approved and applauded weeks before the Budget without it being made clear where the bill is going to fall. There also tends to be an assumption that it is "the other man" who is going to be made to pay for the roads, schools and hospitals which we all feel to be necessary.

It also follows that taxes *as such* do not necessarily raise prices. With a VAT prices of many commodities are 10% higher than they would be without a VAT, but it is not the tax itself which raises prices but the level of government expenditure it is intended to finance. If there were no VAT the revenue would have to be collected in some other way. If (as at present) this was by other taxes falling on goods and services such as purchase tax and SET there is not necessarily any overall difference. If the revenue was collected by an increase in personal income taxes, prices might be that much lower but consumers would have that much less money in their pockets after taxes with which to buy.

Economists classify taxes into direct taxes and indirect taxes. This is a useful distinction, but one we now know to be far less clear cut than was thought by those who devised the terms. Direct taxes are taxes which fall on income and wealth. In the UK this includes income tax and surtax (soon to be replaced by unified tax) corporation tax, capital gains tax, and estate duty. Indirect taxes are applied to expenditure and include Customs and Excise duties, purchase tax, and now VAT. It used to be thought that direct taxes were always actually borne by those who paid them while indirect taxes, even though collected at an intermediate stage in production, were passed forward to the ultimate consumer and were a tax on his expenditure. If you increase income tax in such a way that a particular individual has £100 more to pay, that is £100 less in his pocket. If the Excise duty on whisky is increased so that the blender has to pay more for whisky taken out of bond, no one expects this to be a squeeze of profits of blenders, distributors, retailers and bars. It is expected and intended to be passed forward and reflected in prices to the consumer.

A more rigorous analysis suggests that it is not quite as simple as that. Taxes on incomes, and particularly taxes on companies and other business enterprises, tend to be partially passed forward to the consumer. There is a tendency (no more) for businesses to react to increases in taxation by increasing their gross margins in order to maintain their net after tax profitability. On the other hand increases in *indirect* taxes are not necessarily always passed on to the consumer and sometimes tend to squeeze profit margins. This whole question of "tax incidence" is one of the most difficult and controversial in economic theory.

Social security contributions and SET do not fit neatly into the "direct v. indirect" classification. Social security contributions and particularly graduated pension contributions for individuals are generally regarded as direct taxation. SET also falls on individuals but as Chapter 25 shows the rationale of the tax depends on its being a tax on service which *is* passed forward to the consumer. In substance therefore it is probably best regarded as an indirect tax and this seems to be the view of the present government.

VAT is being introduced in the UK at a rate and coverage which is in general terms intended to replace purchase tax and SET.

It follows that all we are doing is to change the form of our indirect taxes. The case for (and against) so doing is as much a matter of administration as of economics. The first question to be asked is whether VAT is the most efficient form of indirect tax. This is discussed in Chapters 24 and 25.

Some of the economic arguments put forward in favour of VAT such as the suggestions that it is an export incentive or that it leads to a more efficient use of resources are, in general, only valid if it is assumed that VAT be a substitute for *direct* taxes. It is sensible to ask what the effect would be of reducing rates of personal and company direct taxation and replacing the revenue with VAT. Indeed the introduction of VAT in Denmark *was* associated with a reform and reduction of direct taxation. The question has logically to be divided into two parts. First, is VAT the most efficient form of indirect taxation? If it is, would we achieve our policy objectives more efficiently by moving some of the tax burden from direct to indirect taxation? The answer may well be that by introducing a broadly based VAT we make it possible to collect more revenue from indirect taxes than would have been available under purchase tax. This then makes it possible to reduce the burden of direct taxation.

The main argument against direct taxes is that they are taxes on efficiency, on what we put *into* the economy. The man who works harder and earns more money pays more tax. The business which uses scarce capital resources more efficiently and earns a higher rate of return pays more tax. Investors, who really perform the classical role afforded by economic theory to the capital market, making sure that new capital is channelled to those companies who can use it most efficiently for the welfare of all, pay more tax. Productive activity is penalised and may be discouraged. The arguments rage about the dis-incentive effect of taxation: about the only point on which informed opinion is reasonably unanimous is that it is the high *marginal* rates (the extra tax on the extra £ of income) rather than high *average* rates (the ratio of total tax to total income) that do the damage.

In contrast, an indirect tax such as purchase tax or VAT is a tax on what we *take out* of the economy — not on what we produce but on what we consume. Apart from being more efficient it may be more palatable. Most people resent more the tax they pay on an hour's overtime than the tax they pay on a glass of Scotch. The first tax can only be "avoided" by not working. The second can be avoided by not drinking. Indirect taxes, except on necessities, are to this extent voluntary taxes.

For the man who spends all his income there would be little to choose between a flat rate tax on income and flat rate tax on expenditure. If his gross income is £1,000 per annum it is all the same to him whether the government takes 20% at source leaving him with £800 to spend on tax-free goods or whether he is left with the full £1,000 but finds that because of a 25% VAT he can still only buy goods to the tax-free value of £800. Of course no country adopts such an extreme and most levy some taxes at both levels.

Even on the over-simplified and wholly unrealistic assumption of comparing absolutely flat rates of direct and indirect taxation there is still an important economic effect, via savings. Under direct taxation, the man who wants to save part of his income can do so only out of net-of-tax income. He will then have to pay further taxes on the yield he obtains from his savings. If all taxes were collected as indirect taxes he would escape tax completely on any money he saved or spent. Direct taxes are a dis-incentive to saving in the way that indirect taxes are not.

Taxes are *not* typically at flat rates. Under the UK unified tax proposal there will be a single basic rate of tax of 30%. Only those with total incomes in excess of £5,000 or investment income in excess of £2,000 will pay at any other rate. Nevertheless there is a difference between average and marginal rates because of the impact of personal allowances. A married man with no children will pay no tax on the first £775 of his income. If his actual income is £1,500 he will pay £67.50 tax, an average rate of 6.75%. If his income is £2,000 he will pay £367.50, an average rate of 18.38%. In both cases his *marginal* rate, the extra tax on an extra pound of income, will be 30%.

Indirect taxes are not at flat rates either. Until the 1972 Budget, purchase tax rates rose to a maximum of 45% on some goods and there have in the past been 100% rates. The effective rates on alcohol drinks, tobacco and petrol are much higher. On the other hand food bore no tax at all. VAT can in principle be applied at multiple rates and five countries so far have adopted a multiple rate system. Even with the flat rate there are substantial categories of goods and services which enjoy zero rating and certain categories which are still subject to heavy special taxes. We have to discuss therefore the economic effects of the discriminatory features of both direct and indirect taxes.

In broad social and economic terms there are three separate grounds for wanting to build discriminations into our tax system. These are often confused, but rational discussion requires that they be kept distinct.

The first is to discriminate between *individuals*, recognising that those with higher incomes have a greater taxable capacity and can be required to contribute more than their proportionate share to the cost of running public services. At the same time there are the economically underprivileged (including the young, the old and the sick) who cannot only be excused from making a contribution to government expenditure for all of us but who will receive net cash and other benefits from the State. The need for some "discrimination" of this nature is beyond dispute, the main arguments are about how far it is appropriate to carry the principle of taxing those with high incomes and on the most appropriate way of benefiting those with low incomes. The Government's initiative in seeking to replace the present muddle of tax rebates and social welfare benefits with some more consistent and coherent scheme of negative income tax is to be welcomed.

Indeed this initiative and the need for it shows one of the weaknesses of our traditional thinking about taxation in the UK. We tend to want every separate tax to be "fair": if the price of coal goes up, we work out what this will mean to the old age pensioner and argue against the change on such grounds.

We have a system of direct taxation which imposes a higher proportionate as well as a higher absolute burden on those with higher incomes. We have specific benefits for the sick, the old, the unemployed and those with large families. In addition there are a number of income related benefits and subsidies involving rent rebates, free school meals and many other items. The entitlement to certain kinds of social security is also income related. Not content with this we look at the income distribution effect of our indirect taxes. By imposing a higher rate of purchase tax on so-called luxuries we appear to put a higher burden on the rich who can afford such luxuries. By excluding food from the tax base we ease the load on those who have to spend a very high proportion of their income on necessities. On this argument VAT, imposed on a broader base and at a flat rate is "regressive" to use the popular emotive, but technically inaccurate, term. To impose VAT on food as so many countries have done would, on this view, be even worse. On the other hand the tobacco and alcohol taxes bear *relatively* much more heavily on the working man's beer and cigarettes which form a large part of his budget than on the rich man's brandy and cigars on which his expenditure is relatively insignificant. Many of the pleasures of the rich, such as personal servants and expensive holidays abroad, may escape indirect taxation altogether.

A simpler and much more constructive approach is to look at the effect on income distribution of the tax package as a whole. Let us have a simple flat rate of VAT and let the tax fall where it may. Then calculate what the effect will mean on people in different income groups and in different family circumstances. There may for instance prove to be a substantially adverse effect on the low income family with only one earner and five young children. There may be a very favourable effect on a similar family 15 years ahead when the children are grown up, mother and father are both working and the two remaining unmarried sons are going out to work and paying something towards their lodging. We then find the most efficient way of compensating the hard cases out of tax reliefs, or by increases in old age pensions and other welfare benefits. We keep simple as many of our taxes as possible. We concentrate the redistributive aims of society on those taxes, mainly direct taxes, which can most efficiently achieve this end.

Fortunately thanks to the basic statistical data collected by the Family Expenditure Survey and to the work undertaken by Professor C.V. Brown* and published by the Institute for Fiscal Studies we now have more data on the personal effects of tax changes. It is far easier to predict the effects of any tax package on people in a wide range of circumstances and then simultaneously to bring in corrective measures.

There is a straight conflict between redistribution and

*The Impact of Tax Changes on Income Distribution (1972 Edition) C.V. Brown. The Institute for Fiscal Studies. Distributed by Research Publications Victoria Hall East Greenwich London S.E.10. Price £1.20.

incentive. Any attempt to flatten out net after-tax incomes *must* mean imposing high marginal rates of tax on extra income. This is mathematically inevitable. High effective marginal rates of tax affect not only the rich but also those on various forms of income-related national assistance and the problem is a real one. There can be no absolute answer and a political judgment must be taken on the right compromise. At least we can take this judgment on the basis of a complete knowledge of the overall effects. As explained above, having decided on a level of government expenditure we have to decide on the most efficient means of collecting the necessary tax revenue. In the same way, having decided on the pattern of income redistribution we require, we should consider the most efficient tool for *that* purpose. This tool is almost certainly personal direct taxation and social security benefits rather than juggling with rates of VAT and other consumption taxes on a particular commodity.

This then is the case for a flat rate, broadly based VAT in preference to the existing structure of purchase tax or of a complicated multiple rate VAT structure such as is found in France. It *must* be associated with a proper study of the incidence of the tax on people in different circumstances and with compensating changes in personal taxes and social security benefits. On this argument, food too should be included in the base. As an economist I would welcome this but if I were a politician I would certainly shy away from the problem of selling the idea to the electorate. The zero rating of food must be regarded as a political necessity given the state of public opinion and the historical tradition dating back to the disputes over the Corn Laws. There is not much of a pure economic case for it.

There is a second reason for imposing taxes at different rates. This is to discriminate, not between different individuals but different types of consumption by the same individuals. There is also a quite different argument. It is not redistributive but paternalistic and implies that the "gentleman in Whitehall" knows best how the people should spend their money. If we put a high tax on beer, zero rate books and actually subsidise art galleries the State is expressing a value judgment that people should spend less time drinking beer and more time reading and looking at pictures. There is something to be said for this view: personally I enjoy all three but rather resent the idea that politicians and government officials should seek to influence my choice between them. Alcohol and tobacco are very heavily taxed and some moral justification may be put up for that. In fact the main reason for these taxes is the same as that for the extra 10% on motor cars. Experience has proved that these commodities will bear a high rate of tax and are extremely good revenue earners.

On the subsidy and tax exemption level the effects in practice are inconsistent and wholly arbitrary. Under VAT books will be zero rated while theatres, and painters selling their own work will not. Under the old regime if I as a Londoner visit Covent Garden my evening out is subsidised. If I buy a record of the same opera I would suffer purchase tax at a high rate. This might be regarded as subsidising the metropolis at the expense of the regions.

The third argument for discrimination is the "welfare economics" one. Elementary economic theory assumes that individuals will allocate their money between various expenditures and allocate their time between leisure and work in such a way as to maximise their own satisfaction: in general individuals seeking to maximise their own satisfaction will, through the actions of free and competitive markets, tend to bring about the best use of resources in the world as a whole. Undergraduates master this during their first week and spend the rest of their three years learning about the exceptions. The difference between a trained economist and an economic crank is that the crank becomes so bemused by particular exceptions that he forgets all about the basic rule.

One of the exceptions, the classic discussion of which is to be found in Professor Pigou's "Economics of Welfare" first published in 1920, is that individuals, only equate *personal* costs with *personal* benefits in making their decisions.

There are also *social* costs and *social* benefits which he ignores. I am not one for vogue words or consensus. Indeed my personal definition of "consensus" is "the view on a subject taken at a particular time by all informed men of goodwill — except those few who actually understand the subject". It might nevertheless be convenient to explain the concepts of welfare economics in terms of the vogue word of "environment", although this is to tell only part of the story. An industrialist might decide that the best way to power his factory is to burn solid fuel. In this he is considering the private cost. He may give some regard to the fact that he will have a smoking chimney but he might only consider the inconvenience to himself, the extra wear and tear on his own buildings and loss of amenities to his own workers. He will not (the argument runs) consider the effect via the environment on others and the cost that he is imposing on them. Someone who wishes to travel might decide that using his own car is cheaper and more convenient than using public transport. He would not take account of the extra wear and tear he is putting on the roads, which to *him* are free, or that he is adding to congestion and contributing to delays to other road users. Far worse, if he had a noisy sports car or motorcycle the noise may actually amuse him. It is less likely to amuse the thousands of people he disturbs as he speeds past. In cases where the nuisance is not so great as to require prohibition there is a lot to be said for imposing a tax on such activities designed to compensate society for the social costs which they are imposing on other people. On the other hand people with well kept gardens and well painted houses give pleasure to passers-by as well as to themselves and improve the general amenity of the neighbourhood. People who eat sensibly, take medical advice when necessary and generally take steps to maintain their own and their family health benefit society as well as themselves. Such activities should be encouraged if possible by a subsidy.

The only difficulty with this type of argument is that it is in fact very hard to devise the tax or a pricing policy for a public service which meets the test of a rigorous welfare economic analysis. This test is at least as demanding and exacting as that used by a company in making a purely financial capital investment appraisal. Only too often pseudo welfare arguments are put forward by those who have made up their mind what they think would be good by wishful thinking when they are faced with the inadequacy of the financial case. They then invent a spurious "social cost" or "social benefit" which they cannot quantify, but which they argue bridges the gap between hope and reality.

On the whole then it is probably better to impose indirect taxes at a flat rate on a broad base. There would have to be a few exceptions for political reasons and no Government is going to throw away the revenue raising advantages to be gained from taxing alcohol, tobacco and petrol. Redistributive ends are better served through the machinery of direct taxation.

My own view is that there is still scope for increasing somewhat the proportion for taxes collected in UK by VAT by eliminating some of the items at present zero rated or by increasing the rate. Direct taxes on income could then be reduced somewhat. I stress the word "somewhat": I would certainly not advocate pushing this principle too far. I am also sure that it is right to use the chance to get used to a new tax at a relatively modest rate which will have no overall impact on the general level of prices. Once we learn to live with it governments might well consider a further change of emphasis.

24. VAT Versus Other Forms of Indirect Taxation

As I explained in Chapter 23, economists usually divide taxes into "direct taxes" levied on incomes and profits, and "indirect taxes" levied on consumption. An increase in income tax would on the oversimplified classical view actually reduce the net income of the owner of a wholesale business, but an increase in purchase tax would simply be passed on and would not affect his profits.

Much of the confusion in discussing the economic effects of VAT comes from not comparing like with like. There are really two questions. First, is VAT a more efficient form of indirect tax than others? Second, is there a case for financing a larger part of government revenue by indirect taxes? If the answer to both is "Yes", the right strategy is to adopt VAT and eventually to impose it at rates which permit a reduction in direct taxes. For practical reasons it may be advisable to start VAT at relatively low rates until the public are used to it and only later to make the switch of emphasis.

Indirect taxes are mostly used to simply raise revenue. Sometimes, there are other objectives. Higher rates of tax may be imposed on what are thought of as "luxuries", presumed to be bought by the rich, and there may be lower rates or exemptions on food and other so-called necessities.

Higher rates of tax are imposed in most countries on tobacco, alcohol, petrol and certain other items. It can also be argued that the use of tobacco and alcohol is harmful and should be discouraged, or that a high tax on petrol can be regarded as a means of passing part of the cost of maintaining and constructing roads onto those who actually use them. This group of motives gets publicity when taxes are raised, but, to a cynical economist, it is noticeable that tax rates actually imposed tend to be very close to what he might have recommended if he had been asked to advise on how amply to maximise revenue.

There are four basic systems of general indirect taxation: sales tax, purchase tax, cascade turnover tax and value added tax. The simplest in concept is the point-of-sale sales tax imposed at the retail level as a flat percentage on all sales. This is commonly found at State or municipal level in the United States. It is probably the most efficient form of indirect tax economically and has the advantage that it can be applied to services as well as to goods. Its major disadvantage is administrative, because of the vast number of points of collection. Only an advanced country with a highly developed and uncorrupt public service and a good record of taxpayer cooperation could contemplate administering such a tax without the risk of widespread evasion.

The second variation is a purchase tax at the wholesale level such as we still have in the United Kingdom. Here, the point of collection is the point at which the wholesaler sells to the retailer and the tax is based on wholesale prices. It is, of course, added onto the retail price. This considerably reduces the number of points of collection. Because the tax is simple to collect, it becomes more practicable to impose it at different rates on different categories of commodity. The purchase tax imposed at wholesale level has two disadvantages compared to the sales tax imposed at retail level. The first is that it cannot be applied to services which in consequence were relatively undertaxed in the United Kingdom. The second is rather more subtle. The retailer has to finance and take risks on the goods he buys. It is no concern of his whether the price he pays represents the cost of manufacturing, profits of the wholesaler or tax-paid to the Government. He will need a certain percentage mark-up to induce him to stay in business. Although *customary* mark-ups are based on the price, less the purchase tax, in the long run an economic equilibrium mark-up might include purchase tax. There is thus a danger that the cost of the tax to the consumer may be more than the revenue to the Government.

Sales taxes and purchase taxes are normally imposed only

on goods sold to the general public. Goods purchased by businesses are, in general, not taxed, on the grounds that these are eventually to be used in the production of goods that will be taxed. Some items which are used both by businesses and by private individuals may be subject to the taxes because of the administrative difficulty of determining which goods are for which use.

As explained in Chapter 26, other European countries had more general indirect taxes, which could apply to goods sold to other businesses. The old German turnover tax, for instance, was a cascade tax, imposed each time goods changed hands with a cumulative effect. This was obviously both inequitable and inefficient, imposing a far higher effective tax burden on goods which went through several hands in the course of manufacture, and putting a quite irrational premium on vertical integration. It has, therefore, been replaced by a VAT. The cascade turnover tax has nothing in its favour. It is dead and unlikely to be revived.

The practical choice, therefore, is between a purchase tax, a retail sales tax and VAT. On these, purchase tax is administratively the simplest and has the fewest points of collection. Its main weakness is that it is too narrowly based. At its highest rates it can seriously distort consumer choice: it may indeed be favoured by a paternalistically inclined Government for this reason. In spite of these high rates, the narrow base means that it is not particularly powerful as a revenue earner. The exclusion of services can be criticised both by those who (like myself) favour a flat rate non-discriminatory tax covering all forms of consumer expenditure and also by those at the opposite extreme who think that the gentleman in Whitehall knows best and therefore want to place heavy taxes on "luxuries". Rich individuals, like rich countries, tend to spend a high proportion of their disposable income on services.

In broad economic effects there is little to choose between a retail sales tax and VAT. The advantage of VAT is an administrative one. Most sales to the consumer are made through retail outlets which are often relatively small businesses. With a retail sales tax the Government has to rely on these people to collect and pay over the whole of the tax.

With a VAT the retailer is still a point of collection but the greater part of the tax revenue has already been collected at a much smaller number of collection points before the goods pass to the final retail stage. The retailer can only evade tax on his margin and as his inputs are fairly easily ascertained there is limited scope even for that.

Another small advantage of VAT is that it avoids the problem of goods which are used both by businesses and by private individuals. If such goods are exempted there is an unnecessary restriction of the tax base. If they are taxed, there is a small element of double taxation as the tax enters into the cost of production of goods which are again to be taxed. VAT, with its system of credits, neatly avoids this problem.

In the United Kingdom the overwhelming argument for adopting VAT is that this is the system of tax adopted by all our nearest neighbours and trading partners. There is a considerable simplification on imports and export transactions if our systems work in harmony. This would be true even if we did not have an obligation under the EEC Directives to introduce VAT.

25. VAT Versus Selective Employment Tax

Selective Employment Tax was first introduced in the 1966 Budget. A weekly tax was to be collected in respect of all employees. It was refunded (originally with a premium but after a delay), to employers in manufacturing industries. It thus constituted a manufacturing employment *premium* and a non-manufacturing employment *tax*. For a manufacturing industry although there was a promise of a premium there was an immediate cash squeeze because of the delay in making the refund. Given the then state of the economy this was indeed one of the features making the tax attractive to the Government. In its original form the tax was designed to collect £600 million gross and to yield £315 million net after refunds. Subsequently there were two increases in rates and in the last year of the Labour Government the gross collection was of the order of £1,920 million and the net yield £606 million.

There were three good things to be said about SET:

1. SET is an efficient revenue raiser, and (in spite of the apparent nonsense of collecting tax only to pay 68% of it back to the same people) very cheap to collect even expressed as a proportion of the net yield after refunds. Without such a tax it is hard to see how the Labour Government could have forced up the total tax burden from 33% to 44% of Gross National Product during their period of office.

2. There is a case for a general payroll tax as encouraging the efficient use of labour. This argument, if valid, applies with equal force to manufacturing industry as to the service trades. In other words, it would justify the "ET" but not the "S".

3. Services were undertaxed in the UK. Purchase taxes applied at the wholesale level cannot be applied to services, and a VAT or point-of-sale retail tax in other countries does include services. A special tax on employment in the service trades provided a rough and ready, but administratively workable, means of redressing the balance. This argument has nothing to do with efficiency: such a tax *should* (like purchase tax) be passed on to the consumer.

The third point has no necessary connection with the antipathy shown by some politicians and others to services. Economics students are taught in their first term that, although the concepts of "primary", "secondary" and "tertiary" industry are useful distinctions for some purposes all contribute to wealth. Growing cocoa beans, making chocolate bars and distributing them are equally valid parts of the productive process. The final consumer product is the bar on the shop counter and this has a higher value (and cost) than the same bar in the factory warehouse. Consumers in advanced countries invariably spend a higher proportion of their income on services than consumers in poorer countries.

The Industrial Policy Group in an attack on SET drew attention to what they described as "in some quarters a doctrinaire distaste for the service industries and an obstinate conviction that employment in them constitutes national waste" or as Sam Brittain put it at the time, some people "only believe that something is wealth if it hurts when you bump into it". In spite of Professor Kaldor's attempts to put an academically respectable gloss on this heresy, a heresy it remains.

However, although services are as valid an expression of the creation of wealth and of consumer preferences as actual manufactured goods, they are equally suitable as the object of taxation. SET was a rough and ready substitute for a purchase tax which was applied to goods. It was somewhat arbitrary in its impact and as the tax was so much a head, bore more heavily on those service industries employing a lot of cheap labour. The definitions were often odd; even odder than those to be found under VAT.

The Reddaway Report was an astonishingly misconceived

apologia for SET. In his 1970 Budget speech, Mr. Roy Jenkins said:

"The Report shows many of the criticisms of the tax to be unfounded. It shows that in both the retailing and wholesaling sectors of the trade, SET possibly associated with the progressive ending of resale price maintenance, has led to an appreciable increase in productivity in addition to that which would have occurred in any case".

Did the Report in fact reach a conclusion, and to the extent it did, do the arguments put forward stand up to critical analysis? The answer to both questions is no.

In fact the Report showed that "productivity" (as defined) has increased by 11.1% between 1965 and 1968. By a highly sophisticated piece of statistical analysis it suggested that 5.6% of this improvement could be attributed to forces already at work (roughly to a continuation of past trends) leaving a 5.1% residual improvement which must be credited to "SET Effect", again as defined.

The statistics are probably valid, although Professor Reddaway, good statistician that he is, explicitly set out his own doubts and qualifications. The real weakness is to be found in the definitions of "SET Effect" and "Productivity" which do not mean what Mr. Jenkins suggested that they meant. Even if "SET Effect" had led to a 5.1% increase in "Productivity" using the Reddaway definitions, this definitely does *not* mean that the Selective Employment Tax has improved retail efficiency in any ordinary English meaning of the language used.

In the first case the Reddaway Report frequently quoted its own definition: 'the phrase "SET Effect" is shorthand for the effect of all abnormal new factors'. Apart from SET the most important of these factors was that during the period under review Mr. Heath's Act abolishing resale price maintenance was substantially modifying the structure of retail prices, margins and methods. The productivity gain was as likely to derive from this as from SET. The Report chose to define its terms to lump both together under the misnomer "SET Effect".

The second weakness, the definition of "Productivity" is more serious, yet received much less comment at the time.

Reddaway nowhere *explicitly* defined what he means by "productivity" nor did he discuss any possible weakness of this definition on which pages and pages of advanced statistical analysis must rest. "Productivity" is in fact simply assumed to be a ratio between an index of the *volume* of retail sales (that is the value of sales corrected for price changes) and an index of the number of people employed in retailing. If your local grocer reduced his staff from 5 to 4 and stops delivering this represents on the Reddaway approach, a 25% increase in productivity! No account whatsoever is taken of the decline in the *quality* of the service nor of the extra consumer costs borne by the housewife.

Any concept of productivity must be based on a relationship between the value of output and the cost of producing it. If the cost of producing the same model car is reduced (in manpower terms) by increased efficiency there is a clear and easily measurable gain in productivity. If there is a model change and the same manhours go to produce a *better* car there is also a gain in productivity just as tangible but just a little more difficult to measure. This difficulty is fully discussed in the literature on the subject.

Professor Reddaway admitted that it is *"conventional* to measure changes in their" (i.e. the service trades) "output by reference to changes in the volume of goods sold (i.e. by changes in the value of sales when adjustment has been made for changes in price) without making any allowance for changes in the quality of the service (e.g. speedy attention, good selection, offered willingness to grant credit). We have *necessarily* maintained this statistical convention. . . . . . " (my underlinings). The Report devotes two and half pages (126—128) out of 316 to a desultory discussion of this central problem.

Reddaway therefore reached the non-conclusion that "the SET Effect" (defined to include inter alia the effect of the abolition of RPM) has led to an increase in "Productivity" (defined to exclude any changes in the quality of service and this during a period when consumers were becoming free to opt for lower margins/lower service on a wide variety of goods!).

The effect of SET was to raise the cost of providing

services, including retail services. This cost would normally be passed on to the consumer. Assuming that incomes, other prices and tastes remain unchanged if the price of something rises, the consumer will pay less for it. If the tax on whisky is raised, the consumer will drink less whisky. This is *certain* (with one highly technical exception which is rare in practice) but we do not know from first principles whether *expenditure* on whisky will rise or fall. If demand is what economists call inelastic, the proportionate fall in volume consumed will be less than the price rise and expenditure will rise. If demand is elastic, volume consumption will fall proportionately more than the price change and expenditure, as well as consumption, will fall.

It follows that a tax which raises the cost of providing retail services will result in consumers accepting a lower level of services. It does not require a major study by a statistics Professor to tell us that SET raises the price of and reduces the demand for retail services. *Obviously* employment relatively to volume sales will fall. *Obviously*, as the Report admitted on page 192, the quality of service will fall. The interesting question is whether the first obvious fall is greater or less than the second. On this, Reddaway had nothing to say, and concentrated all his statistical big guns on analysing the inevitable.

A tax on whisky which increases (relative) price to the consumer reduces the demand for whisky and employment in the distilling industry. A tax on retail services reduces the demand for them and employment in retailing. If as a result of the first tax whisky sales, and employment in distilling both fell 10%, productivity would be unchanged, and we would not expect otherwise. On the second, Reddaway, looking at one side of the ratio, would conclude that productivity had risen 11.1%!

Services are a perfectly valid object of taxation. If the price of retail services rises and the demand for them falls this is neither better nor worse than similar changes in the price of or demand for anything else that can be bought or sold. If customers stop having their goods delivered by a large store in Knightsbridge and start going in person to the local supermarket, there is a decline in service which the customer presumably thinks is justified by the reduction in price. Thanks to the abolition of r.p.m. (the other identified factor in the miscalled "SET Effect") the consumer has a choice. He can opt for different combinations of price and service, and now has the choice of cut prices on a cash and carry basis which he did not always have before. This is a real widening of consumer choice and if it has resulted in a decline in retail employment relative to sales this reflects consumer preference. If the same decline results from SET this is consumer preference distorted by tax (although as services were previously undertaxed it could be argued that it was a correction of a previous distortion the other way). Neither indicates any change in the efficiency at which a given level of services are provided.

SET incorporated two good ideas, but combined them into a monstrosity with the only real virtue that it is cheap and easy to collect. It may well have led to a slight increase in retail efficiency, but this is not demonstrated by the Reddaway Report. Professor Reddaway "proved" his point by defining his terms, Humpty Dumpty fashion, to mean what he wanted them to mean. He set a trap for careless readers who may be deluded into thinking that "SET Effect" means the effect of SET and that "gain in productivity" means improvement in efficiency.

VAT in comparison is a straight unpretentious tax on services as well as goods with no claims to any particular influence on consumption, the distribution of income, consumer choice or efficiency.

Some of the material in this Chapter was previously published in "The Spectator" of 25th April, 1970.

26. The Experience of Other Countries

As explained in Chapter 24, there is little economic difference between a Value Added Tax and the type of purchase tax familiar in the United Kingdom or the sales tax levied at point-of-sale and found (at the State or Provincial level) in the United States and Canada. To understand the enthusiasm of the Common Market countries for VAT one must compare it with the economically inefficient cascade turnover tax.

This Chapter gives a brief account of the history of Value Added Taxation in the six original members of the Common Market, plus the Scandinavian countries and Ireland. It is not intended either as a full description or a detailed comparative analysis of the indirect tax systems of these countries. This information can be found in other sources, such as Volume 4 of the loose leaf service "Guide to European Taxation", published in English by the International Bureau of Fiscal Documentation in Amsterdam. I have attempted to draw attention to interesting features found in some countries and to give some indication of what problems were met and how they were dealt with.

Both Germany and France introduced a turnover tax shortly after the 1914—18 War. Initially, the German tax was at a rate of ½% on turnover with no credit for taxes paid at previous stages. Where the consumer purchased goods which had been entirely produced or manufactured in one organisation, the effective tax burden was ½%. If the goods had passed through six different organisations the rate of tax would reach 3%. (In practice the rate would not be quite as high as that because of the profit element at each stage). A tax at this rate is unlikely materially to distort competition and the structure of industry, but after the Second War the rate of tax at each stage rose to 4%. The difference in the total tax burden to the final consumer of goods which had gone through several stages rather than one then did become material and distorted competition. There was very strong pressure towards vertical integration and against specialisation. Various special reliefs were given, for instance to wholesalers, and certain vertically integrated firms in industries such as textiles where specialisation was the norm were subjected to taxes at higher rates. In spite of these somewhat arbitrary measures the position was obviously unsatisfactory.

Another difficulty with the German type of turnover tax concerns exports. Foreign customers simply do not pay United Kingdom purchase tax or American or Canadian sales tax. Exempting them is a simple procedure. The only administrative complication concerns goods sold by retail to foreign visitors, and a fairly satisfactory procedure has been set up for this. In the case of a cumulative turnover tax, goods exported will have borne tax at earlier stages and this tax will have been passed on to customers, whether at home or abroad, in the price. To compensate for this the final exporter was given a refund which purported to neutralise the tax element in the goods he was selling. This had two disadvantages. First of all, calculations were inevitably complicated and arbitrary resulting, in spite of a considerable administrative load, in under-compensation in some cases and over-compensation in others. Under-compensation is a deterrent to exports while over-compensation would be in breach of GATT and might be attacked by foreign competitors.

In any case, because there was an actual payment to the final exporter, foreign competitors often accused Germany of subsidising her exporters, even in cases where the charge was not justified and it was very hard to produce detailed and convincing evidence sufficient to refute this suspicion. Certainly, multi-stage cascade turnover taxes are very difficult to reconcile with the type of free trade, ignoring frontiers, which is one of the first objectives of the European Economic Community.

France, too, started with a multi-stage turnover tax but reacted more quickly than Germany to the problems created. In 1926 a single stage purchase tax was introduced in addition to the cascade taxes. This proved complicated and in 1936 there was substituted a production tax which, again in principle, was a single stage tax. There was an exemption for goods which were being used in further productive processes which should in principle have removed the objections to the multi-stage turnover tax. However, there was no exemption for capital goods (which discriminated against physical investment) and there was no remission for exports.

In 1948 France took another step in the direction of a Value Added Tax. This was the introduction of a fractional tax permitting traders to offset tax borne on goods they had purchased against tax due on the goods they sold. In 1955 this credit was extended to the purchase of capital goods, thus creating a true tax on value added (TVA) similar in substance to but in practice rather different from the present system.

In particular, the French system was only a true value added tax up to the wholesale level. It did not extend to the retail stage of distribution, nor, on the whole, did it tax services which by their nature are essentially "retail". Separate taxes were imposed at these stages thus detracting from the simplicity of the system. In addition, full relief was not given for capital inputs.

The European Economic Community was conceived of as much more than a customs union and one of the subjects obviously requiring attention was tax harmonisation. The first major report on this subject was the Neumark Report of 1962 which made recommendations for the harmonisation of both direct and indirect taxes. Very little progress has been made towards unifying tax systems as far as they concern the taxation of personal income and wealth and of corporate profits. Indeed of the three main types of corporation tax, that recommended by Neumark is now the least likely to be adopted.

The harmonisation of indirect taxes was obviously more urgent. There is little point in abolishing tariffs while there are incompatible systems of taxing turnover and sales. To take a simple example, if it were decided to abolish purchase tax in Scotland, people living in the North of England would have tended to do their shopping in Scotland and this could only be prevented by maintaining customs barriers. There are also subtle ways in which indirect tax systems could be used as a form of protection for local industries thus defeating the purpose of the customs union. The administrative savings and convenience of a customs union would disappear if frontier barriers had to be kept in being to deal with border tax anomalies.

After much discussion, the Commission of EEC published two Directives both dated 11th April, 1967 proposing the introduction in all member states of a common system of taxes on value added. This system is to be more far reaching and consistent than the French tax on which it was modelled. In particular it would in principle be extended to the retail stage and full credit would be given for capital inputs. There was no requirement that the tax should be levied at a uniform rate or that there should be uniform product categories in cases where more than one rate was levied. An English translation of the Directives is given in Appendices 3 and 4. The first draft of the first Directive was originally submitted by the Commission to the Council of Ministers on 5th November, 1962. The second Directive had its origins in 1965, but was finally approved simultaneously with the first.

The Directives required member countries to introduce the tax by 1st January, 1970. The first countries to comply were France and Germany on 1st January, 1968. In the case of France, the change was, of course, less far reaching and required less adjustment because of the similarity of the existing system. The necessary extension to the retail stage was in fact a complication, but this was matched by a substantial reduction in the previously long list of exemptions and special cases. The quick reaction from Germany was for the opposite reason. The German cascade turnover tax had obviously been in need of reform for some time and this had only been held up pending a Community decision on the basis for harmonisation.

Value Added Tax was introduced into the Netherlands on 1st January, 1969, Luxembourg on 1st January, 1970 and Belgium on 1st January, 1971. The Belgians had been given a year's extension by the further Directive of 9th December, 1969 (Appendix 5). This Directive gave Italy an extension to

1st January, 1972 but this deadline was also missed. Recently introduction of the tax has been postponed yet again by six months from 1st July next to 1st January, 1973.

The convenience of having the same basic system of indirect taxes as one's neighbours and trading partners is obvious and several other European countries, not members of the EEC and not in any way bound by the Directive, took steps to introduce VAT. Denmark indeed (3rd July, 1967) was, in fact, ahead of any of the EEC members. In her case, it was part of the far reaching general reform of the tax structure and coincided with the introduction of a form of PAYE. This was followed by Sweden (1st January, 1969), and Norway (1st January, 1970).

TABLE. Effective Rates of VAT in Various Countries

	Date of Introduction	Standard Rate	Low Rate	Intermediate Rate	High Rate
Belgium	1. 1.1971	18	6	14	25
Denmark	3. 7.1967	10	—	—	—
	1. 4.1968	12.5	—	—	—
	29. 6.1970	15	—	—	—
France	1. 1.1968	20	6.383	14.92	25
	1.12.1968	23.456	7.526	19.647	33.33
	1. 1.1970	23	7.5	17.60	33.33
Germany	1. 1.1968	10	5	—	—
	1. 7.1968	11	5.5	—	—
Ireland (proposed)	1.11.1972	16.37	5.26	—	30.26
Luxembourg	1. 1.1970	10	5	—	—
Netherlands	1. 1.1969	12	4	—	—
	1. 1.1971	14	4	—	—
Norway	1. 1.1970	20	—	—	—
Sweden	1. 1.1969	11.11	—	—	—
	1. 1.1971	17.65	—	—	—

The table shows the date of introduction of the tax in the various countries and the rates adopted. It will be seen that there are still a wide variety of rates because of the different emphasis which different tax systems place on the direct and indirect taxation and different levels of public expenditure. The old EEC countries have found it necessary to differentiate between different categories of goods. The three Scandinavian countries have a single rate, an example we have followed.

Sweden is now alone expressing the tax at a "tax inclusive" rate. In all the other countries tax is expressed as a percentage of the invoiced price *exclusive* of tax. In Sweden the rate is expressed as 15% of the invoice price *including* the tax itself. As the following calculation shows, this is equivalent to a rate of 17.65% on the tax exclusive rate and for consistency of comparison this is the figure shown in the table.

Price net of VAT	85
VAT	15
Price inclusive of VAT	100

The tax of 15 is 17.65% expressed as a percentage of 85.

France, too, originally calculated VAT on a tax inclusive basis. On 1st January, 1970 a change was made to a tax exclusive basis to simplify administration. New rates were set to be more or less equivalent to the old tax inclusive rates.

Although in Sweden there is, in principle, a single rate, the effect of a reduced rate is given in certain cases by reducing the taxable *base* and applying the single rate to the reduced rate. This is, of course, equivalent to applying a reduced rate on a full base. The taxable base of buildings is reduced by 40% and for certain public works by 80%. It is said that the object of this is to achieve neutrality. If individuals or local authorities employed direct labour for buildings they would save VAT on the labour content and in the absence of special measures, they would be discouraged from using contractors. A reduced rate leaves the contractor in substantially the same position. Of course, the full rate of tax could have been charged by treating anyone who built his own house as a taxable person subject to tax on a self delivery (see Chapter 7). This might have been difficult to enforce and doubtless there are also economic or social reasons for the concession. Again, to preserve neutrality, it has been necessary to impose a lower *rate* on the import of prefabricated houses. This rate is 9% VAT inclusive, equivalent to 9.39% VAT exclusive.

Similarly, in the United Kingdom, there is to be an additional 10% car tax (as well as the normal 10% VAT) on home produced and imported cars. This is consistent with the continuation of extra taxes on tobacco and alcohol.

The postponement of the introduction of the tax in Belgium from 1970 to 1971, was partly based on the experience of the Netherlands where there had been a sharp rise in prices. At the time the prices were in any case rising rapidly and it was felt that VAT would simply add to this tendency. The contrasting experience of Germany had shown the advantage of introducing the tax at a time when the economy was going through a mild deflationary period. The difficulties of Belgium were made rather worse by the considerably lower level of taxpayer compliance to be found in that country. The problems were shown up in an anti-VAT trademen's strike in February, 1971. It was complete and impressive: I was there.

The delays in Italy have been due in part to changes in Government, weaknesses in administration and the attempt to introduce a complete package of tax reforms including particular income tax. It also appears that in Italy it is really true that rebates given to exporters over-compensated for the cascade taxes imposed at earlier stages (see Chapter 24). There was a real, rather than just an apparent, element of export subsidy in the Italian system. With the introduction of VAT this would disappear and hence exporters have been unenthusiastic about the change.

The Italians have also apparently argued the theoretically correct point that a Value Added Tax is in economic terms a second best to a single point-of-sales tax. This contrasts oddly with the point often made in the United Kingdon and the United States that a retail sales tax would be more appropriate to the Anglo-Saxon countries with their sophisticated and uncorrupt administrations and the law-abiding attitude of their citizens. The extra complexities of a Value Added Tax are (it is said) only really necessary to deal with the special problems of enforcement in the Latin countries. Given that they *need* to have such a tax for administrative reasons it is more convenient, the argument continues, for their trading partners to follow their example. The Italian arguments in favour of an eventual sales tax also contrasts oddly with their plea that it is very difficult for them to extend the VAT to the retail stage as required by the EEC Directives.

Ireland is to introduce VAT with a three rate system designed initially to reproduce the effective rates of sales tax. The start originally planned for 1st January, 1972 was first postponed until 1st March. The new target date is 1st November.

Appendix 1
The White Paper

This is the text of the Government's White Paper Cmnd 4929 published on 21st March, 1972. The "Appendix" referred to was the draft Clauses in the Finance Bill. These are given, as actually published in the Bill on 11th April, 1972 in Appendix 2. The Bill is subject to amendment by Parliament.

VALUE ADDED TAX

1. In his Budget Speech last year the Chancellor of the Exchequer announced that, as from April 1973, both SET and purchase tax will be abolished and a value added tax will become operative. He explained that the replacement of our present system of selective taxation by a broad based value added tax will produce a much fairer system of indirect taxation. A Green Paper was also published then as a basis for comprehensive discussions about the administration and other details of the tax.

2. Detailed discussions have since been held with trade and industry on the basis of the Green Paper. Customs and Excise officials have also visited other countries with a VAT in operation and have studied their systems at first hand. These discussions have been of great value, and in the light of them decisions have been taken on the structure and coverage of a VAT best suited to the needs and circumstances of the United Kingdom. The Chancellor in his Budget Statement today has announced the proposed coverage of the tax and confirmed that it will come into effect on 1st April 1973 when the remaining SET and purchase tax will be abolished. Draft Clauses and Schedules for the Finance Bill are set out in the Appendix to this White Paper for the information of Parliament and the public. Changes in numbering and arrangement as well as drafting changes may need to be made when the Clauses and Schedules come to be incorporated in the Finance Bill. In substance, however, they represent the Chancellor's proposals as they will appear in that Bill.

3. One of the major objectives in planning the VAT, widely shared by the many trade representatives who have been consulted, has been to keep it simple. VAT is now in full operation in eight countries. We have been able to benefit from their experience and the system which has been prepared for this country is much more simple than most. VAT is essentially a wide-ranging tax on consumer expenditure. Proposals for introducing deviations from the basic outline of the tax have therefore had to be subjected to extremely critical appraisal. In particular, it has been concluded that the introduction of more than one rate, in addition to being open to many of the objections which apply to the present multi-rate structure of purchase tax, would create excessive problems of administration for all concerned. The VAT system which is now

proposed is as simple as is practicable in the circumstances of this country.

4. *Coverage of the tax.* VAT will be chargeable at a single standard rate on the supply of all goods and services in the United Kingdom in the course of a business and on all imports of goods, except where the legislation makes specific provision to the contrary. Exceptions to tax at the standard rate may take the form of either exemption or zero-rating. These terms are explained in paragraphs 10 and 11.

5. Exports will be zero-rated; so too will food (except those items now liable to purchase tax and " meals out "), books, newspapers (including newspaper advertising) and journals, coal, gas, electricity, petrol, the construction of buildings, fares for public transport, and drugs and medicines supplied on prescription. Full details are shown in Schedule 4 in the Appendix. Exemption will apply to land, insurance, letter and parcel post, betting and gaming (which already bear excise duty), finance, education and health services. The details are set out in Schedule 5 in the Appendix. There is provision for the Schedules to be modified by Treasury Order.

6. *Level of standard rate.* The Chancellor's intention is that the standard rate at the inception of the tax should be 10 per cent, and Clause 9 in the Appendix provides for this. In order to allow for the needs of economic management, however, the Clause also permits this initial rate to be altered, by Treasury Order made before 1st April 1973, to a rate in the range $7\frac{1}{2}$ per cent to $12\frac{1}{2}$ per cent.

7. *Motor cars.* The Chancellor has announced that, when VAT becomes operative, there will also be a separate tax on new and imported motor cars at the rate of 10 per cent of the wholesale value. This, together with VAT, will result in a slight reduction in the tax element in the retail price of motor cars.

8. *The VAT system.* In principle value added tax is, as its name implies, a tax which is paid by each trader on the value which he adds to any goods (or services) during his particular stage of the process of production or distribution. But although the tax is collected from traders at each stage, it is in final effect a tax on consumers' expenditure. Just as the value of the goods (or services) at the point of supply to the final consumer represents the sum of all the values added by successive traders, so the final tax which is paid by the consumer represents the sum of all VAT paid by successive traders. But, because each trader pays only the VAT attributable to the value added at his stage, it does not matter how many stages there are in the process: for any given final value, the final tax is the same. Thus VAT is quite different from a " cascade " tax, where tax is charged on the turnover at each stage so that the more stages there are, the bigger the tax bill at the end of the line.

9. *The " value added ".* In practice a trader will not be required to calculate his actual value added. Instead, whenever he buys a product or service to which the standard rate of VAT applies, he will pay his supplier tax at this rate on his purchase. When in turn he supplies such goods or services to his own customers he will charge them tax at the standard rate on his sales. At regular intervals, when he has to make a return to Customs and Excise, he will add up first all the tax he has paid his suppliers in the period (his " input tax ") and then all the tax he has charged his customers on his sales in the same period (his " output tax "); the difference is the amount which he will pay to Customs and Excise. If in any period his " input tax " is greater than his " output tax "—perhaps because he is stocking up, or has made a purchase of an expensive piece of equipment—then at the end of that period he will be entitled to a refund of tax from Customs and Excise.

10. *Exemption.* Where goods or services are exempt (see Schedule 5 in the Appendix), the trader does not have to charge his customer any " output tax ". Unless he has other business which is taxable, he does not have to keep records

and he does not have to account for any tax to Customs and Excise; on the other hand, he is not entitled to take credit for, or to reclaim, any tax included in the price of his purchases.

11. *Zero-rating.* A trader selling zero-rated goods or services also does not have to charge tax to his customers. But unlike the trader in exempt goods or services he sells them entirely tax free because he can reclaim any " input tax " which he may have paid to his suppliers. Thus, because exports are zero-rated, an exporter may reclaim any tax paid at earlier stages in respect of goods he exports.

12. *Exemption for small traders.* Small traders will be exempt from VAT. For this purpose a small trader is one whose business turnover in taxable supplies of goods or services (including zero-rated supplies) does not exceed £5,000 a year: detailed provisions are in Schedule 1 in the Appendix. Traders who qualify for this exemption will not be required to register with Customs and Excise. They will pay a tax-inclusive price when they buy in goods or services, but they will not be required to keep VAT records or to charge and account for tax on the supplies which they themselves make: conversely no question of any relief from input tax will arise. Small traders may, however, be allowed to register voluntarily if their business is such that this will be to their advantage, and if they register they will, of course, have to keep records and accounts like other registered traders.

13. *Records and accounts.* All persons (including companies and partnerships) whose turnover in taxable supplies of goods or services (including zero-rated supplies) is above £5,000 will be required to be registered with Customs and Excise and to account for tax on their own transactions. When such a taxable person supplies goods or services in the United Kingdom, he will have to keep a record of the VAT chargeable on them and, if the supply is to another taxable person, to issue him with a " tax invoice " showing the amount of tax charged and other particulars.

14. To avoid unnecessary changes in business systems, records and accounts will not need to be kept in any particular prescribed form, and will be based on normal purchase and sales invoice records, coupled with a record of all operations affecting the business's VAT liability (e.g. receipts of taxable goods or services; supplies by the business; credits allowed to or by the business). The tax invoice issued in respect of each taxable supply to a taxable person will, again, not be in a prescribed form, but as well as giving particulars relating to the tax charge (description, quantity and price of goods or services, and rate and amount of VAT) it will need to contain other details necessary to establish its validity, to identify the supplier and the customer, and to show when the tax became due on the supply.

15. *Returns of tax.* At the end of each accounting period, every taxable person will be required to make a return of tax payable to Customs and Excise, or repayable to him, for that period. As is explained in paragraph 9, he will pay over to Customs and Excise the difference between his output tax and his input tax, and where the input tax in any accounting period comes to more than the output tax, Customs and Excise will repay the difference. Thus, once credit has been taken for input tax, any goods held in stock become effectively free of tax pending their sale. A typical trader, who charges more tax to his customers in an accounting period than he pays on purchases from his suppliers, will be liable to pay the difference over to Customs and Excise only at the end of the period, and to this extent VAT has the effect of increasing somewhat the liquidity of traders overall.

16. The standard accounting period will be three months, with a month's grace for paying the quarter's net tax, and accounting periods will be so allocated

that about one-third of the total number of three-monthly returns will be due each month. When, however, a taxable person expects that his input tax will regularly exceed his output tax (for example, because he is an exporter and most of his outputs are zero-rated) he will be eligible for a shorter accounting period of one month so that he may obtain earlier repayments. The quarterly or monthly return form will be sent to the taxable person at the appropriate time by Customs and Excise, and will ask for information about tax due and tax deductible, together with particulars of the value of outputs in each tax category and of taxable inputs.

17. *Registration.* The process of registration will start in October 1972. Full publicity will be given to the arrangements nearer the time. Those liable to register will then be able to obtain from Customs and Excise leaflets explaining the tax in detail and a copy of the form on which they will need to make their notification. There will be provision for considerable flexibility in regard to registration of companies. For example, a group of associated companies may apply to be registered as one trader for VAT purposes, and it will be possible for a company to apply to have its various divisions registered separately.

18. *Partial exemption.* Most traders will be wholly inside or outside the scope of the tax. But where part of a taxable person's business is in exempt supplies and part is in taxable supplies, some allocation of input tax between the two types of output will be necessary. If, say, only half of a trader's outputs are taxable, only half the input tax may be deducted. (This simple formula will not, however, be appropriate to every case.) At the end of each accounting period the partly exempt trader will determine the amount of input tax which he may deduct for that period. This deduction will be provisional; at the end of the year the amount of deductible input tax will be determined finally in the light of his trading pattern for the year, as shown by his periodical returns, and any overpayment or underpayment of tax resulting from the provisional calculation will be adjusted. In order to simplify accounting, there is provision in Clause 3 in the Appendix for dispensing with allocating input tax between taxable and exempt supplies in cases where the trader's exempt outputs are not significant.

19. *Special schemes for retailers.* Even with the basically simple tax structure that is proposed, accounting problems are bound to arise for some businesses in so far as they deal in goods liable at both standard rate and zero rate. In order to simplify the administration for these businesses, enabling powers are included in Clause 30 in the Appendix to allow special methods of accounting for the tax by retailers in cases where it would be unduly difficult for them to operate the normal rules. There will be a range of special methods allowing output tax on sales of goods to be assessed by reference to purchases in each tax category, thus avoiding the need for detailed records of outputs to be kept. Information about these schemes is being made available to interested trade associations.

20. *Special scheme for local authorities, etc.* Local authorities' business activities will generally be treated in the same way as those of ordinary traders. However, their welfare and other non-business activities will be outside the scope of the tax and VAT falling on any purchases by them of goods and services for these activities will not be deductible under the normal credit mechanism. In order to avoid the tax on these purchases burdening the rates or rate support grant, special arrangements will be made under Clause 15 in the Appendix for the tax to be refunded by Customs and Excise.

21. *Second-hand goods.* In general, there will be no special rules for second-hand goods, and the consideration for a sale of such goods by a taxable person in the course of his business will be chargeable with VAT in the ordinary way.

There is, however, provision in Clause 14 in the Appendix for a special scheme to be introduced in exceptional cases (e.g. cars, where it is appropriate for the tax to be assessed on a different basis; details will be worked out in discussion with representatives of the trades concerned.

22. *Capital goods.* After careful consideration of various schemes for the special tax treatment of the acquisition or disposal of capital goods, it has been decided that any advantages such schemes might have are unlikely to justify the work and form-filling that they would involve. No special rules are therefore proposed, though there is power to introduce them later if they prove to be needed. When a capital asset is acquired by a taxable trader, the input tax paid on it will be treated in the same way as any other input tax: it will attract an immediate credit in the accounting period in which the tax invoice is received. And when capital goods are disposed of, they will be treated like other second-hand goods sold in the course of business, the value of the disposal being included in the total value of the trader's taxable supplies in the period in question.

23. *Imports.* Administratively, VAT payable on importation will generally be treated in the same way as customs duty, except that Clause 18 in the Appendix empowers the Commissioners of Customs and Excise to make regulations allowing taxable persons to take delivery of imported goods without at that time paying the tax chargeable. Wholly taxable persons will be allowed to account for import VAT by entering it in their ordinary output tax account, and at the same time to claim an input tax deduction of the same amount. The effect will be that the two items cancel each other in the return for the accounting period in question. Of course, when the point of subsequent sale or disposal is reached, output tax will be chargeable in the normal way.

24. *Self-supply and transfers to personal use.* Under Clause 5 in the Appendix a supply of goods or services will normally involve a transaction between two persons. There are, however, two cases in which a supply will be deemed to result from the action of a single person. The first is where a taxable person uses goods stocked or produced by his business for private purposes (whether of himself or someone else): Schedule 2 in the Appendix provides that such applications to personal use shall be taxable. The other may occur if an exempt or partly exempt business decides to supply its incidental needs from its own resources (for example, to print its own stationery) rather than by purchasing them from outside, when it would have to pay input tax which would be non-deductible. This may result in significant distortion of competition against the normal suppliers of the goods or services involved, and the Treasury will then be able, under the power in Clause 6 in the Appendix, to make an Order treating the self-supply as taxable. If the trader concerned is, or becomes, registered, output tax will then be payable on the value of the supply, but a deduction of the tax paid on inputs to it may be claimed. It is intended that an Order of this kind should be made in respect of stationery, operative from the start of the tax.

25. *Non-deductible inputs.* All countries with a VAT have found it necessary to restrict the right to claim credit for tax on inputs in the case of certain goods and services, in particular those which are likely to be used for both business and private purposes. Clause 3 in the Appendix gives enabling powers to apply similar restrictions. These powers will be utilised from the start of the tax only in respect of business cars and business entertaining (other than that provided for overseas customers).

26. *Appeal machinery.* In the event of a dispute about the tax between a trader and Customs and Excise, it is important that there should be an easy and inexpensive method of resolving the dispute as quickly as possible. Clause 40 and Schedule 6 in the Appendix therefore provide for a system of independent VAT tribunals to which persons affected by the tax will be able to appeal if they think that the decision of Customs and Excise on any of the matters listed

in Clause 40 is open to challenge. The tribunals will be the sole judges of fact on any matter referred to them, but an appeal will lie from their decision on points of law to the ordinary Courts.

27. *Transitional arrangements for retail and other stocks.*

(*a*) *Goods chargeable with purchase tax.* The Chancellor of the Exchequer, in his Budget Statement today, referred to the problem of stocks held by retailers and other traders which have borne purchase tax and which, if unsold when VAT is introduced, will attract VAT as well. He has proposed that those traders dealing in the goods listed below should, by agreement with Customs and Excise, use sale or return arrangements so that goods remaining unsold when VAT is introduced and purchase tax abolished will be free of purchase tax. Such arrangements are already widely used, with for example motor cars, and they work satisfactorily.

	Purchase tax groups
Furs and fur goods	1(*b*), 2(*b*), 8(*a*), 9(*b*)(i)
Jewellery (real or imitation), clocks and watches, and precious metal articles of personal adornment	4(*a*) and (*b*), 17
Domestic appliances and apparatus (except the non-electric non-gas bottom rate goods)	12(*b*) to (*e*)
Radio and television receivers, valves, loudspeakers	18
Musical instruments, gramophones	19(*a*) and (*b*)
Gramophone records	19(*c*)
Tape recorders/reproducers	19A(*a*)
Tapes and containers	19A(*b*) and (*c*)
Cameras, enlargers and projectors	24(*a*) and (*b*)
Road vehicles	27
Hair waving and hair drying machines	30(*c*)

For other goods, it is proposed to remove purchase tax by Order a short time before VAT is introduced. This will provide traders with a period within which to dispose of stocks on which purchase tax has been charged and to build up stocks which have not borne purchase tax in preparation for the introduction of VAT. The precise timing will be announced nearer the date of the changeover.

(*b*) *Goods chargeable with revenue duties.* The extent to which a duty-paid stocks problem may arise in the case of alcoholic drinks, tobacco, matches and mechanical lighters will depend on whether the revenue duties on these goods are altered when VAT, to which they will also be liable, is introduced; this in turn will depend on the total revenue required from these duties in 1973–74. As the Chancellor of the Exchequer announced in his Budget Speech, he proposes to take power to make any appropriate reduction in these duties by Treasury Order; in that event, the date of the change will be so arranged as to provide a similar solution for stocks as is envisaged for purchase tax. No stocks problem arises with hydrocarbon oils since these will be zero-rated under VAT.

28. *Further action.* Customs and Excise are ready to continue the consultations they have been having with representative trade bodies about the detailed operation of the tax, and to give advice and guidance on any problems connected with it. Later this year steps will be taken to ensure that traders are aware of their liability to register and of the need to notify Customs and Excise of the fact. Customs and Excise will make available comprehensive literature

explaining what has to be done, both for reg stration and subsequently. Different blocks of traders will be asked to notify by different dates, starting from 1st October 1972, so as to provide a steady flow of registrations and to ensure that all those liable to registration are in fact registered before April 1973. Those who would like any further information about VAT requirements should consult their local Customs and Excise office.

Appendix 2
The Finance Bill, 1972

A

B I L L

TO

Grant certain duties, to alter other duties, and to amend the law relating to the National Debt and the Public Revenue, and to make further provision in connection with Finance.

A.D. 1972

Most Gracious Sovereign,

WE, Your Majesty's most dutiful and loyal subjects, the Commons of the United Kingdom in Parliament assembled, towards raising the necessary supplies to defray Your Majesty's public expenses, and making an addition to the public revenue, have freely and voluntarily resolved to give and grant unto Your Majesty the several duties hereinafter mentioned; and do therefore most humbly beseech Your Majesty that it may be enacted, and be it enacted by the Queen's most Excellent Majesty, by and with the advice and consent of the Lords Spiritual and Temporal, and Commons, in this present Parliament assembled, and by the authority of the same, as follows:—

PART I

VALUE ADDED TAX

Imposition and extent of tax

1.—(1) A tax, to be known as value added tax, shall be Value added charged in accordance with the provisions of this Part of this tax. Act on the supply of goods and services in the United Kingdom (including anything treated as such a supply) and on the importation of goods into the United Kingdom.

(2) The tax shall be under the care and management of the Commissioners, who may do all such acts as may be deemed necessary and expedient for raising, collecting, receiving and accounting for the tax in like manner as they are authorised to do with relation to any duties under their care and management.

(3) All money and securities for money collected or received for or on account of the tax shall—

(a) if collected or received in Great Britain, be placed to the general account of the Commissioners kept at the 1952 c. 44. Bank of England under section 11 of the Customs and Excise Act 1952 ;

(b) if collected or received in Northern Ireland, be paid into the Consolidated Fund of the United Kingdom in such manner as the Treasury may direct.

1920 c. 67. (4) The Government of Ireland Act 1920 shall have effect as if the tax were one of the taxes mentioned in section 22(1) of that Act (reserved taxes).

1968 c. 2. (5) The Provisional Collection of Taxes Act 1968 shall be amended by inserting in subsection (1) of section 1, after the words " income tax ", the words " value added tax " ; and the Act as so amended shall apply in relation to a resolution of the House of Commons passed before 1st April 1974 and providing for any variation of that tax as it applies in relation to such a resolution as is mentioned in subsection (2)(a) of that section.

Scope of tax. **2.**—(1) Except as otherwise provided by this Part of this Act the tax shall be charged and payable as follows.

(2) Tax on the supply of goods or services shall be charged only where—

(a) the supply is a taxable supply ; and

(b) the goods or services are supplied by a taxable person in the course of a business carried on by him ;

and shall be payable by the person supplying the goods or services.

(3) Tax on the importation of goods shall be charged and payable as if it were a duty of customs.

(4) Any reference in the following provisions of this Part of this Act to the supply by any person of goods or services is a reference to such a supply in the United Kingdom in the course of a business carried on by him.

3.—(1) The following tax (in this Part of this Act referred to as " input tax "), that is to say—

Deduction of input tax.

(a) tax on the supply to a taxable person of any goods or services for the purpose of a business carried on or to be carried on by him ; and

(b) tax paid or payable by a taxable person on the importation of any goods used or to be used for the purpose of a business carried on or to be carried on by him ;

may, at the end of any prescribed accounting period, be deducted by him, so far as not previously deducted and to the extent and subject to the exceptions provided for by or under this section, from the tax chargeable on supplies by him (in this section referred to as " output tax ").

(2) Where the amount of input tax that may be so deducted by any person exceeds the amount of the output tax due from him, the amount of the excess shall be paid to him by the Commissioners.

(3) Subject to subsection (6) of this section, the input tax that may be deducted by a taxable person shall be—

(a) the whole of that tax, if all his supplies of goods or services are taxable supplies ; and

(b) such part of that tax as, in accordance with regulations under this section, is attributable to taxable supplies, if some but not all of his supplies of goods or services are taxable supplies ;

and any such regulations may provide for treating all supplies of goods or services by any person as taxable supplies where the tax attributable to exempt supplies would be less than such amount or less than such part of the whole of the tax as may be specified in the regulations or in such other circumstances as may be so specified.

(4) The Commissioners shall make regulations for securing a fair and reasonable attribution of input tax to taxable supplies, and any such regulations may provide for—

(a) determining a proportion of supplies in any prescribed accounting period which is to be taken as consisting of taxable supplies ; and

(b) provisionally attributing input tax in accordance with the proportion so determined and adjusting the attribution for periods comprising two or more prescribed accounting periods or parts thereof ;

and may make different provision for different circumstances and, in particular (but without prejudice to the generality of this provision) for different descriptions of goods or services ; and may contain such incidental and supplementary provisions as appear to the Commissioners necessary or expedient.

(5) Regulations under this section may include provision for enabling a taxable person to deduct as input tax, in such cir-

cumstances, to such extent and subject to such conditions as may be specified in the regulations, tax on the supply to him, or paid by him on the importation, of goods notwithstanding that he was not a taxable person at the time of the supply or payment.

(6) The Treasury may by order make provision for excepting from the preceding provisions of this section input tax chargeable on such supplies and importations as may be specified in the order, and any such provision may be framed by reference to the description of goods or services supplied or goods imported, the persons by whom they are supplied or imported or to whom they are supplied, the purposes for which they are supplied or imported, or any circumstances whatsoever ; and any such order may contain provision for consequential relief from output tax.

Taxable
persons.

4.—(1) A person who makes or intends to make taxable supplies is a taxable person while he is or is required to be registered under this Part of this Act.

(2) Schedule 1 to this Act shall have effect with respect to the registration of persons under this Part of this Act.

Supply

Supply of
goods and
services.

5.—(1) The following provisions apply for determining for the purposes of this Part of this Act what is a supply of goods or services.

(2) Supply of goods includes all forms of supply and, in particular, the letting of goods on hire and the making of a gift or loan of goods ; but supply of services does not include anything done otherwise than for a consideration.

(3) Where a person produces goods by applying to another person's goods a treatment or process he is treated as supplying the goods so produced and not as supplying services.

(4) The supply of any form of power, heat, refrigeration or ventilation is a supply of goods and not of services.

(5) Schedule 2 to this Act shall have effect with respect to matters to be treated as a supply of goods.

Finance

(6) The granting, assignment or surrender of a major interest in land shall be treated as a supply of goods.

In this subsection " major interest " means the fee simple or a tenancy for a term certain exceeding twenty-one years, and, in relation to Scotland, means the estate or interest of the proprietor of the *dominium utile,* or in the case of land not held on feudal tenure, the estate or interest of the owner, or the lessee's interest under a lease for a period exceeding twenty-one years.

(7) Subject to the preceding provisions of this section, the Treasury may by order provide with respect to any description of transaction—

(a) that it is to be treated as a supply of goods and not as a supply of services ; or

(b) that it is to be treated as a supply of services and not as a supply of goods ; or

(c) that it is to be treated as neither a supply of goods nor a supply of services.

(8) Subject to the preceding provisions of this section, anything which is not a supply of goods but is done for a consideration (including, if so done, the granting, assignment or surrender of the whole or part of any right) is a supply of services.

6.—(1) The Treasury may by order make provision for Self-supply. securing, with respect to such descriptions of goods as may be specified in the order, that, subject to any exceptions provided for by or under the order, any such goods which are acquired or produced by a person in the course of a business carried on by him and—

(a) are neither supplied to another person nor incorporated in other goods produced in the course of that business ; but

(b) are used by him for the purpose of a business carried on by him ;

are treated for the purposes of this Part of this Act as both supplied to him for the purpose of that business and supplied by him in the course of that business.

(2) The Treasury may by order make provision for securing, with respect to services of any description specified in the order, that, where—

(a) a person, in the course of a business carried on by him, does anything for the purpose of that business which is not a supply of services but would, if done for a consideration, be a supply of services of a description, specified in the order ; and

(b) such other conditions as may be specified in the order are satisfied ;

such services are treated for the purposes of this Part of this Act as being both supplied to him for the purpose of that business and supplied by him in the course of that business.

(3) For the purposes of this section, where goods are manufactured or produced from any other goods those other goods shall be treated as incorporated in the first-mentioned goods.

Time of supply.

7.—(1) The following provisions of this section shall apply for determining the time when a supply of goods or services is to be treated as taking place for the purposes of the charge to tax.

(2) Subject to the following provisions of this section, a supply of goods shall be treated as taking place—

(a) if the goods are to be removed, at the earlier of the following, that is to say—

(i) the time of the removal ; and

(ii) the expiration of the period of three months beginning with the time when the goods are made available to the person to whom they are supplied ;

(b) if the goods are not to be removed, at the time when they are made available to the person to whom they are supplied ;

except that if, before the time applicable under paragraph (a) or paragraph (b) of this subsection, the person supplying the goods provides such a tax invoice in respect of the supply as is required under section 30(2) of this Act (or would be so required if the person to whom the goods are supplied were a taxable person) the supply shall, to the extent covered by the invoice, be treated as taking place at the time the invoice is issued.

(3) Where goods are deemed to be supplied by virtue of paragraph 1 of Schedule 2 to this Act or section 6 of this Act, the supply shall be treated as taking place when they are applied or used as mentioned in that paragraph or section.

(4) The Commissioners may by regulations make provision with respect to the time at which a supply of goods is to be treated as taking place in cases where goods are supplied for a consideration the whole or part of which is determined or payable periodically or at the end of any period or at the time the goods are appropriated for any purpose, and any such regulations may provide for treating goods supplied on hire for any period as being successively supplied on hire for successive parts of that period.

(5) Subject to subsection (6) of this section, a supply of services shall be treated as taking place at the time when the services are performed, except that if before that time the person supplying the services issues an invoice or receives a payment in respect of the supply, the supply shall, to the extent covered by the invoice or payment, be treated as taking place at the time the invoice is issued or the payment is received.

(6) The Commissioners may by regulations make provision with respect to the time at which a supply of services is to be treated as taking place in cases where services are supplied for a consideration the whole or part of which is determined or payable periodically or at the end of a period, and any such regulations may provide for treating services supplied for any period as being successively supplied for successive parts of that period.

8.—(1) The following provisions of this section shall apply Place of for determining, for the purposes of the charge to tax, whether supply. goods or services are supplied in the United Kingdom.

(2) If the supply of any goods does not involve their removal from or to the United Kingdom they shall be treated as supplied in the United Kingdom if they are in the United Kingdom and otherwise shall be treated as supplied outside the United Kingdom.

(3) If the supply of any goods involves their removal from the United Kingdom they shall be treated as supplied in the

United Kingdom and if it involves their removal to the United Kingdom they shall be treated as supplied outside the United Kingdom.

(4) Subject to subsection (5) of this section, if services might be considered as supplied either in or outside the United Kingdom or as supplied both in and outside the United Kingdom, they shall be treated as supplied in the United Kingdom if the person supplying them has his place of business or principal place of business in the United Kingdom and otherwise shall be treated as supplied outside the United Kingdom; but for the purposes of this subsection any person carrying on a business through a branch or agency in the United Kingdom shall be treated as having his principal place of business in the United Kingdom.

(5) Where services consist of transport between places of which one is and the other is not in the United Kingdom, so much of the services as consists of transport within the United Kingdom shall be treated as supplied in the United Kingdom and the remainder as supplied outside the United Kingdom.

(6) The Treasury may by order make provision, with respect to such services as may be specified in the order, for substituting for the provisions contained in subsection (4) or (5) of this section such other provisions as may be specified in the order, either generally or in such circumstances as may be so specified.

(7) Where a supply of goods is such that subsections (2) and (3) of this section cannot be applied to it, subsections (4) and (6) of this section shall apply to it as they apply to a supply of services.

(8) For the purposes of this section, where goods, in the course of their removal from a place in the United Kingdom to another place in the United Kingdom, leave and re-enter the United Kingdom the removal shall not be treated as a removal from or to the United Kingdom.

Rate of tax and determination of value

Rate of tax.

9.—(1) Subject to the following provisions of this section, tax shall be charged at the rate of ten per cent., and shall be charged—

    (a) on the supply of goods or services, by reference to the value of the supply as determined under this Part of this Act; and

    (b) on the importation of goods, by reference to the value of the goods as determined under this Part of this Act.

(2) The Treasury may by order made before 1st April 1973 substitute for the rate of ten per cent. a rate not lower than seven and a half per cent. nor higher than twelve and a half per cent.

(3) The Treasury may by order increase or decrease the rate for the time being in force by such percentage thereof, not exceeding 20 per cent., as may be specified in the order, but any such order shall cease to be in force at the expiration of a period of one year from the date on which it takes effect, unless continued in force by a further order under this subsection.

(4) In relation to an order made under subsection (3) of this section to continue, vary or replace a previous order, the reference in that subsection to the rate for the time being in force is a reference to the rate that would be in force if no order under that subsection had been made.

10.—(1) For the purposes of this Part of this Act the value of any supply of goods or services shall be determined as follows.

(2) If the supply is for a consideration in money its value shall be taken to be such amount as, with the addition of the tax chargeable, is equal to the consideration.

(3) If the supply is not for a consideration or is for a consideration not consisting or not wholly consisting of money, the value of the supply shall be taken to be its open market value.

(4) Where a supply of any goods or services is not the only matter to which a consideration in money relates the supply shall be deemed to be for such part of the consideration as is properly attributable to it.

(5) For the purposes of this Part of this Act the open market value of a supply of goods or services shall be taken to be the amount that would fall to be taken as its value under subsection (2) of this section if the supply were for such consideration in money as would be payable by a person standing in no such relationship with any person as would affect that consideration.

(6) This section has effect subject to Schedule 3 to this Act.

11. For the purposes of this Part of this Act the value of any imported goods shall be taken to be the aggregate of the following, that is to say,—

(a) the amount that would fall to be taken as their value under section 258 of the Customs and Excise Act 1952 if value added tax were a duty of customs; and

(b) the amount of any customs duty payable on the goods or of any payment or repayment made in order to secure relief from such customs duty under section 35 or section 36 of the Customs and Excise Act 1952 (relief on re-importation); and

(c) any amount payable on the goods by way of surcharge under section 7 of the Sugar Act 1956 or a levy under section 1 of the Agriculture and Horticulture Act 1964 or payable on the goods under section 6(5) of the European Communities Act 1972 or that section as applied by section 7(1) of that Act.

Reliefs

12.—(1) Where a taxable person supplies goods or services and the supply is zero-rated, then, whether or not tax would be chargeable on the supply apart from this section,—

(a) no tax shall be charged on the supply; but

(b) it shall in all other respects be treated as a taxable supply;

and accordingly the rate at which tax is treated as charged on the supply shall be nil.

(2) A supply of goods or services is zero-rated by virtue of this subsection if the goods or services are of a description for the time being specified in Schedule 4 to this Act or the supply is of a description for the time being so specified.

(3) Where goods of a description for the time being specified in Schedule 4 to this Act, or of a description forming part of a description of supply for the time being so specified, are imported into the United Kingdom no tax shall be chargeable on their importation, except as otherwise provided in that Schedule.

(4) The Treasury may by order vary Schedule 4 to this Act by adding to or deleting from it any description or by varying any description for the time being specified in it.

(5) Where a description included in Schedule 4 to this Act (whether by virtue of an order under the preceding subsection or otherwise) is of a supply of goods or services outside the United Kingdom or of a transaction which would not otherwise be a supply of goods or services the supply or transaction shall for the purposes of this Part of this Act be treated as a supply of goods or services in the United Kingdom.

(6) A supply of goods is zero-rated by virtue of this subsection if the Commissioners are satisfied that the person supplying the goods : —

    (a) has exported them ; or

    (b) has shipped them for use as stores on a voyage or flight to an eventual destination outside the United Kingdom, or as merchandise for sale by retail to persons carried on such a voyage or flight in a ship or aircraft.

(7) The Commissioners may by regulations make provision for the zero-rating of supplies of goods, or of such goods as may be specified in the regulations, in cases where the Commissioners are satisfied that the goods have been or are to be exported and such other conditions, if any, as may be specified in the regulations or the Commissioners may impose are fulfilled.

(8) Where the supply of any goods has been zero-rated in pursuance of regulations made under the preceding subsection and—

    (a) the goods are found in the United Kingdom after the date on which they were alleged to have been or were to be exported ; or

    (b) any condition specified in the regulations or imposed by the Commissioners is not complied with ;

and the presence of the goods in the United Kingdom after that date or the non-observance of the condition has not been authorised for the purposes of this subsection by the Commissioners, the goods shall be liable to forfeiture under the Customs and Excise Act 1952 and the tax that would have been chargeable on the supply but for the zero-rating shall become payable forthwith by the person to whom the goods were supplied or by any person in whose possession the goods are found in the United Kingdom ; but the Commissioners may, if they think fit, waive payment of the whole or part of that tax.

1952 c. 44.

13.—(1) A supply of goods or services is an exempt supply Exemptions.
5 if it is of a description for the time being specified in Schedule 5
to this Act.

(2) The Treasury may by order vary that Schedule by adding
to or deleting from it any description of supply or by varying
any description of supply for the time being specified in it.

10   **14.**—(1) The Treasury may by order make provision for secur- Relief on supply of certain second-hand goods.
ing a reduction of the tax chargeable on the supply of goods
of such descriptions as may be specified in the order in cases
where no tax was chargeable on a previous supply of the goods
and such other conditions are satisfied as may be specified in
15 the order or as may be imposed by the Commissioners in pursuance of the order.

(2) The amount of the reduction that may be secured by an
order under this section shall not exceed the amount of tax that
would have been chargeable on the previous supply had tax
20 been chargeable on it.

(3) An order under this section may make different provision
for goods of different descriptions and for different circumstances.

  15.—(1) Subject to the following provisions of this section, Refund of tax in certain cases.
25 where tax is chargeable on the supply of goods or services to,
or on the importation of goods by, a body to which this section
applies and the supply or importation is not for the purpose of
any business carried on by the body, the Commissioners shall,
on a claim made by the body at such time and in such form
30 and manner as the Commissioners may determine, refund to
it the amount of the tax so chargeable.

(2) Where goods or services so supplied to or imported by
the body cannot be conveniently distinguished from goods or
services supplied to or imported by it for the purpose of a
35 business carried on by it, the amount to be refunded under
this section shall be such amount as remains after deducting
from the whole of the tax chargeable on any supply to or importation by the body such proportion thereof as appears to the
Commissioners to be attributable to the carrying on of the
40 business; but where the tax so attributable is or includes tax
attributable, in accordance with regulations under section 3 of
this Act, to exempt supplies by the body and the tax attributable
to the exempt supplies is in the opinion of the Commissioners
an insignificant proportion of the tax so chargeable they may
include it in the tax refunded under this section.

(3) The bodies to which this section applies are—

    (*a*) a local authority ;

    (*b*) a river authority, a river purification board, the Con-
        servators of the River Thames and the Lee Conservancy
        Catchment Board ;

1930 c. 44.   (*c*) a drainage board within the meaning of the Land
        Drainage Act 1930 ;

(d) any statutory water undertakers within the meaning of the Water Act 1945, and a regional water board and water development board within the meaning of the Water (Scotland) Act 1967 ;

(e) a passenger transport authority or executive established under Part II of the Transport Act 1968 ;

(f) a port health authority constituted under Part I of the Public Health Act 1936, and a port local authority and joint port local authority constituted under Part X of the Public Health (Scotland) Act 1897 ;

(g) a police authority and the Receiver for the Metropolitan Police District ;

(h) a development corporation within the meaning of the New Towns Act 1965 or the New Towns (Scotland) Act 1968, a new town commission within the meaning of the New Towns Act (Northern Ireland) 1965 and the Commission for the New Towns ;

(i) a general lighthouse authority within the meaning of Part XI of the Merchant Shipping Act 1894 ;

(j) the British Broadcasting Corporation ;

(k) Independent Television News Limited ; and

(l) any body specified for the purposes of this section by an order made by the Treasury.

(4) No tax shall be refunded under this section to a general lighthouse authority which in the opinion of the Commissioners is attributable to activities other than those concerned with the provision, maintenance or management of lights or other navigational aids.

(5) References in this section to any tax chargeable do not include any tax which, by virtue of an order under section 3(6) of this Act, could not be deducted as input tax.

(6) In this section " local authority " means the council of a county, borough, county district, district, parish or group of parishes, community or group of communities, the Greater London Council, the Common Council of the City of London, the Council of the Isles of Scilly, and any joint committee or joint board established by two or more of the foregoing and, in relation to Scotland, the council of a county, county of a city, large burgh, small burgh, district and any combination and any joint committee or joint board established by two or more of the foregoing.

16.—(1) The Treasury may by order make provision for Relief from giving relief from the whole or part of the tax chargeable on tax on the importation of goods, subject to such conditions (including importation conditions prohibiting or restricting the disposal of or dealing of goods. with the goods) as may be imposed by or under the order, if and so far as the relief appears to the Treasury to be necessary or expedient, having regard to any international agreement or arrangements.

(2) The Commissioners may by regulations make provision for remitting or repaying, if they think fit, the whole or part of the

tax chargeable on the importation of any goods which are shown to their satisfaction to have been previously exported from the United Kingdom.

(3) The Commissioners may by regulations make provision for remitting or repaying the whole or part of the tax chargeable on the importation of any goods if they are satisfied that the goods have been or are to be re-exported and they think fit to do so in all the circumstances and having regard to the tax chargeable on the supply of like goods in the United Kingdom.

Further provisions as to importation of goods

17.—(1) Subject to the provisions of this section, the Customs and Excise Act 1952 and, except where the contrary intention appears, any other enactments (including provisions of regulations or other instruments having statutory effect) relating to customs generally, whether passed or made before or after the passing of this Act, shall have effect, with such exceptions and adaptations as the Commissioners may by regulations prescribe, as if all goods imported into the United Kingdom were liable to duties of customs and as if those duties included value added tax chargeable on the importation of goods.

Application of customs enactments. 1952 c. 44.

(2) The following provisions of the Customs and Excise Act 1952, that is to say—

> (a) sections 34(4), 35 and 36 (reimportation);
>
> (b) section 37 (importation of goods from the Channel Islands);
>
> (c) section 43(a) (relief from duty of antiques);
>
> (d) section 221(2) (exemption of certain mechanical lighters);
>
> (e) section 259 (charge of duty on manufactured or composite articles);
>
> (f) section 260(1)(b) (declaration as to duty payable);
>
> (g) section 272 (supply of goods without payment of duty to Her Majesty's ships); and
>
> (h) sections 308 to 311 (Isle of Man);

shall be excepted from the enactments which are to have effect as mentioned in subsection (1) of this section.

(3) Section 258(1) of the Customs and Excise Act 1952 shall have effect, in its application by virtue of subsection (1) of this section, in a case where paragraph (b) or (c) of section 11 of this Act applies, as if the value to be taken as the value of imported goods were increased by the amount mentioned in that paragraph.

1953 c. 36.

(4) Regulations under section 16 of the Post Office Act 1953 (which provides for the application of customs enactments to postal packets) may make special provision in relation to value added tax.

Importation of goods by taxable persons.

18. The Commissioners may by regulations make provision for enabling goods imported by a taxable person in the course of a business carried on by him to be delivered or removed, subject to such conditions or restrictions as the Commissioners

157

may impose for the protection of the revenue, without payment of the tax chargeable on the importation, and for that tax to be accounted for together with the tax chargeable on the supply of goods or services by him.

Special cases

Application to Crown.

19.—(1) This Part of this Act shall apply in relation to taxable supplies by the Crown as it applies in relation to taxable supplies by taxable persons.

(2) Where the supply by a Government department of any goods or services does not amount to the carrying on of a business but it appears to the Treasury that similar goods or services are or might be supplied by taxable persons in the course of a business, then, if and to the extent that the Treasury so directs, the supply of those goods or services by that department shall be treated for the purposes of this Part of this Act as a supply in the course of a business carried on by it.

(3) For the purposes of this section goods or services obtained by one Government department from another Government department shall be treated, if and to the extent that the Treasury so directs, as supplied by that other department and similarly as regards goods or services obtained by or from the Crown Estate Commissioners.

(4) In this section " Government department " includes a department of the Government of Northern Ireland, any body of persons exercising functions on behalf of a Minister of the Crown, and any part of a Government department (as defined in the foregoing) designated for the purposes of this subsection by a direction of the Treasury.

20.—(1) A local authority which makes taxable supplies is Local liable to be registered under this Part of this Act, whatever the authorities. value of the supplies ; and accordingly Schedule 1 to this Act shall apply, in a case where the value of the taxable supplies made by a local authority in any period of one year is £5,000 or less, as if that value exceeded £5,000.

(2) In this section " local authority " has the same meaning as in section 15 of this Act.

21.—(1) Where, under the following provisions of this section, Groups of any bodies corporate are treated as members of a group any companies. business carried on by a member of the group shall be treated as carried on by the representative member, and—

(a) any supply of goods or services by a member of the group to another member of the group shall be disregarded ; and

(b) any other supply of goods or services by or to a member of the group shall be treated as a supply by or to the representative member ; and

(c) any tax paid or payable by a member of the group on the importation of any goods shall be treated as paid or payable by the representative member ;

and all members of the group shall be liable jointly and severally for any tax due from the representative member.

(2) An order under section 6 of this Act may make provision for securing that any goods or services which, if all the members of the group were one person, would fall to be treated under that section as supplied to and by that person, are treated as supplied to and by the representative member.

(3) Two or more bodies corporate resident in the United Kingdom are eligible to be treated as members of a group if—

 (a) one of them controls each of the others ; or

 (b) one person (whether a body corporate or an individual) controls all of them ; or

 (c) two or more individuals carrying on a business in partnership control all of them.

(4) Where an application to that effect is made to the Commissioners with respect to two or more bodies corporate eligible to be treated as members of a group, then, from the beginning of a prescribed accounting period they shall be so treated, and one of them shall be the representative member, unless the Commissioners refuse the application ; but they shall not refuse it unless it appears to them necessary to do so for the protection of the revenue.

(5) Where any bodies corporate are treated as members of a group and an application to that effect is made to the Commissioners, then, from the beginning of a prescribed accounting period—

 (a) a further body eligible to be so treated shall be included among the bodies so treated ; or

 (b) a body corporate shall be excluded from the bodies so treated ; or

 (c) another member of the group shall be substituted as the representative member ; or

 (d) the bodies corporate shall no longer be treated as members of a group ;

unless the application is to the effect mentioned in paragraph (a) or paragraph (c) above and the Commissioners refuse the application ; but they shall not refuse it unless it appears to them necessary to do so for the protection of the revenue.

(6) Where a body corporate is treated as a member of a group as being controlled by any person and it appears to the Commissioners that it has ceased to be so controlled, they shall, by notice given to that person, terminate that treatment from such date as may be specified in the notice.

(7) An application under this section with respect to any bodies corporate must be made by one of those bodies or by the person controlling them and must be made not less than ninety days before the date from which it is to take effect, or at such later time as the Commissioners may allow.

(8) For the purposes of this section a body corporate shall be taken to control another body corporate if it is that body's holding company within the meaning of the Companies Act 1948 ; and an individual or individuals shall be taken to control a body corporate if he or they, were he or they a company, would be that body's holding company within the meaning of that Act.

1948 c. 38.

22.—(1) The registration under this Part of this Act of persons carrying on a business in partnership may be in the name of the firm ; and no account shall be taken, in determining whether goods or services are supplied to or by such persons, of any change in the partnership or of a change from the business being carried on by a person on his own to its being carried on by him in partnership or from the business being carried on in partnership to its being carried on by one of the former partners on his own.

(2) Subsection (1) of this section shall not affect the extent to which, under section 9 of the Partnership Act 1890, a partner is liable for tax owed by the firm ; but where a person is a partner in a firm during part only of a prescribed accounting period his liability for tax on the supply by the firm of goods or services during that accounting period shall be such proportion of the firm's liability as may be just. 1890 c. 39.

23.—(1) The registration under this Part of this Act of a body corporate carrying on a business in several divisions may, if the body corporate so requests and the Commissioners see fit, be in the names of those divisions.

(2) The Commissioners may by regulations make provision for determining by what persons anything required by or under this Part of this Act to be done by a person carrying on a business is to be done where a business is carried on in partnership or by a club or association the affairs of which are managed by its members or a committee or committees of its members.

(3) The Commissioners may by regulations make provision for persons who carry on a business of a taxable person who has died or become bankrupt or incapacitated to be treated for a limited time as taxable persons, and for securing continuity in the application of this Part of this Act in cases where persons are so treated.

24.—(1) Where a person who is accountable for any tax, or on whom any duties are imposed by or under this Part of this Act, is not resident in the United Kingdom, the Commissioners may by notice in writing served on any agent, manager or factor who is resident in the United Kingdom and has acted on behalf of that person in matters by reference to which that person is accountable or the duties are imposed, direct that he shall be substituted for that person as the person accountable for the tax or that he shall be under an obligation to discharge those duties or any of them.

(2) For the purposes of this Part of this Act goods imported by a taxable person and supplied by him as agent for a person who is not a taxable person may be treated as imported and supplied by the taxable person as principal.

(3) Where goods or services are supplied through an agent who acts in his own name the Commissioners may, if they think fit, treat the supply both as a supply to the agent and as a supply by the agent.

25. Where a business carried on by a taxable person is transferred to another person as a going concern, then—

    (a) for the purpose of determining whether the transferee is liable to be registered under this Part of this Act he shall be treated as having carried on the business before as well as after the transfer; and supplies by the transferor shall be treated accordingly; and

    (b) any records relating to the business which, under section 34 of this Act, are required to be preserved for any period after the transfer shall be preserved by the transferee instead of by the transferor, unless the Commissioners, at the request of the tranferor, otherwise direct.

26.—(1) The Treasury may by order make provision for modifying the provisions of this Part of this Act in their application to dealings on terminal markets and such persons ordinarily engaged in such dealings as may be specified in the order, subject to such conditions as may be so specified.

(2) Without prejudice to the generality of subsection (1) of this section, an order under this section may include provision—

    (a) for zero-rating the supply of any goods or services or for treating the supply of any goods or services as exempt;

    (b) for the registration under this Part of this Act of any body of persons representing persons ordinarily engaged in dealing on a terminal market and for disregarding such dealings by persons so represented in determining liability to be registered under this Part of this Act, and for disregarding such dealings between persons so represented for all the purposes of this Part of this Act;

    (c) for refunding, to such persons as may be specified by or under the order, input tax attributable to such dealings on a terminal market as may be so specified;

and may contain such incidental and supplementary provisions as appear to the Treasury to be necessary or expedient.

(3) An order under this section may make different provision with respect to different terminal markets and with respect to different commodities.

27.—(1) Where goods subject to a duty of customs are supplied while warehoused and before payment of the duty the supply shall be disregarded for the purposes of this Part of this Act.

(2) Where goods subject to a duty of excise or such goods mixed with goods subject to a duty of customs are supplied while warehoused and before payment of the duty, then—

    (a) if there is more than one such supply any but the last such supply shall be disregarded for the purposes of this Part of this Act; and

(b) the supply or, if more than one, the last such supply shall be treated for the purposes of this Part of this Act as taking place when the duty is paid and the value of the supply shall be treated as including the duty ; and

(c) the tax on the supply shall be payable, together with the duty, by the person by whom the duty is paid, except as otherwise provided by regulations under this section.

(3) The Commissioners may by regulations make provision for enabling goods which are supplied as mentioned in subsection (2) of this section, and are so supplied to a taxable person for the purpose of a business carried on by him, to be removed from warehouse without payment of the tax on the supply and for that tax to be accounted for together with the tax chargeable on the supply of goods or services by him.

(4) Subsection (1) of this section applies in relation to a surcharge under section 7 of the Sugar Act 1956 or any amount 1956 c. 48. payable under section 6(5) of the European Communities Act 1972 or that section as applied by section 7(1) of that Act as it applies in relation to a duty of customs.

28.—(1) The Treasury may by order make provision for the Capital goods. giving of relief, in such cases, to such extent and subject to such exceptions as may be specified in the order, from tax paid on the supply or importation for the purpose of a business carried on by any person of machinery or plant or any specified description of machinery or plant in cases where that tax or part of that tax cannot be deducted under section 3 of this Act and such other conditions are satisfied as may be specified in the order.

(2) Without prejudice to the generality of subsection (1) of this section, an order under this section may provide for relief to be given by deduction or refunding of tax and for aggregating or excluding the aggregation of value where goods of the same description are supplied or imported together.

(3) An order under this section may substitute a period exceeding three years but not exceeding six years as the period for which records relating to goods in respect of which relief is given under the order may be required to be preserved under section 34(3) of this Act.

Trading stamp schemes.
29. The Commissioners may by regulations make provision for modifying section 10 of this Act and paragraph 5 of Schedule 3 to this Act in their application to the supply of goods under trading stamp schemes within the meaning of the Trading Stamps Act 1964 or the Trading Stamps Act (Northern Ireland) 1965.

1964 c. 71.
1965 c. 6 (N.I.).

Collection and enforcement

Accounting for and payment of tax.
30.—(1) Tax on the supply of goods or services shall be accounted for and paid by reference to such periods (in this Part of this Act referred to as " prescribed accounting periods ") at such time and in such manner as may be determined by or

under regulations made by the Commissioners; and claims for deduction of input tax or for payments under section 3(2) of this Act shall be made in such manner as may be so determined.

(2) Regulations under this section may require the keeping of accounts and the making of returns in such form and manner as may be specified in the regulations and may require taxable persons supplying goods or services to other taxable persons to provide them with invoices (to be known as " tax invoices ") containing statements of such particulars as may be so specified of the supply, the tax chargeable on it and the persons by and to whom the goods or services are supplied.

(3) Regulations under this section may make special provision for such taxable supplies by retailers of any goods or of any description of goods or of services or any description of services as may be determined by or under the regulations and, in particular,—

(a) for permitting the value which is to be taken as the value of the supplies in any prescribed accounting period or part thereof to be determined, subject to any limitations or restrictions, by such method or one of such methods as may have been described in any notice published by the Commissioners in pursuance of the regulations and not withdrawn by a further notice or as may be agreed with the Commissioners; and

(b) for determining the proportion of the value of the supplies which is to be attributed to any description of supplies; and

(c) for adjusting that value and proportion for periods comprising two or more prescribed accounting periods or parts thereof.

(4) Regulations under this section may make provision—

(a) for treating tax chargeable in one prescribed accounting period as chargeable in another such period; and

(b) for the adjustment of accounts in cases where tax has become chargeable by reference to a consideration and the amount of the consideration is reduced or no consideration becomes payable and in such other circumstances as may be specified in the regulations; and

(c) for the correction of errors.

(5) Regulations under this section may make different provision for different circumstances and may provide for different dates as the commencement of prescribed accounting periods applicable to different persons.

(6) The provisions made by regulations under this section for cases where goods are treated as supplied by a taxable person by virtue of paragraph 2 of Schedule 2 to this Act may require the tax chargeable on the supply to be accounted for and paid, and particulars thereof to be provided, by such other person and in such manner as may be specified by the regulations.

(7) Where, at the end of a prescribed accounting period, the

amount of tax due from any person or the amount due to any person under section 3(2) of this Act would be less than £1 that amount shall be treated as nil.

31.—(1) Where a taxable person has failed to make any returns required under this Part of this Act or to keep any documents and afford the facilities necessary to verify such returns or where it appears to the Commissioners that such returns are incomplete or incorrect they may assess the amount of tax due from him to the best of their judgment and notify it to him.

Power of Commissioners to assess tax due.

(2) An assessment under subsection (1) of this section of an amount of tax due for any prescribed accounting period shall not be made after the later of the following:—

    (a) two years after the end of the prescribed accounting period ; or

    (b) one year after evidence of facts, sufficient in the opinion of the Commissioners to justify the making of the assessment, comes to their knowledge ;

but may, where further such evidence comes to their knowledge after the making of such an assessment, be made in addition to that assessment.

(3) Where a taxable person has acquired or imported any goods in the course of a business carried on by him the Commissioners may require him from time to time to account for the goods ; and if he fails to prove that the goods have been or are available to be supplied by him or have been lost or destroyed they may assess to the best of their judgment and notify to him the amount of tax that would have been chargeable in respect of the supply of the goods if they had been supplied by him.

(4) An assessment under subsection (1) or subsection (3) of this section shall not be made more than six years after the end of the prescribed accounting period or importation concerned, except for the purpose of recovering tax lost to the Crown through the fraud or wilful default or neglect of any person.

(5) Where an amount has been assessed and notified to any person under subsection (1) or subsection (3) of this section it shall, subject to the provisions of this Part of this Act as to appeals, be deemed to be an amount of tax due from him and may be recovered accordingly, unless, or except to the extent that, the assessment has subsequently been withdrawn or reduced.

Power to require security and production of evidence.

32.—(1) The Commissioners may, as a condition of allowing or repaying any input tax to any person, require the production of such documents relating to the tax as may have been supplied to him and may, if they think it necessary for the protection of the revenue, require such security as a condition of making any payment under section 3(2) of this Act as appears to them appropriate.

(2) Where it appears to the Commissioners requisite to do so for the protection of the revenue they may require a taxable

person, as a condition of his supplying goods or services under a taxable supply, to give security, or further security, of such amount and in such manner as they may determine, for the payment of any tax which is or may become due from him.

33.—(1) Tax due from any person shall be recoverable as a debt due to the Crown.

(2) Any amount shown in an invoice as tax chargeable on a supply of goods or services shall be recoverable as tax due from the person issuing the invoice, whether or not—

(a) the invoice is a tax invoice issued in pursuance of section 30(2) of this Act ; or

(b) that or any amount of tax is chargeable on the supply ; or

(c) the person issuing the invoice is a taxable person.

(3) The Commissioners may by regulations make provision for authorising distress to be levied on the goods and chattels of any person refusing or neglecting to pay any tax due from him or any amount recoverable as if it were tax due from him, and for the disposal of any goods or chattels on which distress is levied in pursuance of the regulations.

(4) In the application of the preceding subsection to Scotland, for the reference to the levying of distress on goods and chattels there shall be substituted a reference to the doing of diligence, and for the expression " chattels " there shall be substituted a reference to corporeal movables.

34.—(1) Every taxable person shall keep such records as the Commissioners may require.

(2) The Commissioners may by regulations make provision for enabling the Commissioners, in cases where it appears to them necessary to do so for the protection of the revenue, to require persons who supply goods or services but are not required to be registered under this Part of this Act to keep such records as the Commissioners may require.

(3) The Commissioners may require any records kept in pursuance of this section to be preserved for such period not exceeding three years as they may require.

(4) The duty under this section to preserve records may be discharged by the preservation of the information contained therein by such means as the Commissioners may approve ; and where that information is so preserved a copy of any document forming part of the records shall, subject to the following provisions of this section, be admissible in evidence in any proceedings, whether civil or criminal, to the same extent as the records themselves.

(5) The Commissioners may, as a condition of approving under subsection (4) of this section any means of preserving information contained in any records, impose such reasonable requirements as appear to them necessary for securing that the information will be as readily available to them as if the records themselves had been preserved.

(6) A statement contained in a document produced by a computer shall not be admissible in evidence by virtue of subsection (4) of this section unless the conditions mentioned in subsection (2) of section 5 of the Civil Evidence Act 1968 or 1968 c. 64. in the corresponding Scottish enactment are satisfied in relation to the statement and the computer ; and the other provisions of that section and subsections (1), (2), (3) and (5) of section 6 of that Act (supplementary provisions) and the like provisions of the corresponding Scottish enactment shall, with the necessary modifications, apply in relation to the giving of evidence in pursuance of this section.

(7) Notwithstanding the preceding provisions of this section, in criminal proceedings the court may, for special cause, require oral evidence to be given of any matter of which evidence could ordinarily be given by means of a certificate under section 5(4) 1968 c. 64. of the Civil Evidence Act 1968 or under the corresponding Scottish enactment as applied by the preceding subsection.

(8) In subsections (4) and (6) of this section "document", "copy" and "computer" have the same meanings as, by virtue of section 10 of the Civil Evidence Act 1968, they have in Part I of that Act or as they have in the corresponding Scottish enactment.

(9) For the purposes of this section—

1968 c. 70.

    (a) section 13 of the Law Reform (Miscellaneous Provisions) (Scotland) Act 1968 is the corresponding Scottish enactment to section 5 of the Civil Evidence Act 1968 and the provisions of the said section 13 (which are identical in number with the provisions of the said section 5) shall apply accordingly ;

    (b) section 14 of the Law Reform (Miscellaneous Provisions) (Scotland) Act 1968 is the corresponding Scottish enactment to subsections (1), (2), (3) and (5) of section 6 of the Civil Evidence Act 1968 ; and

    (c) section 17 and Part III of the Law Reform (Miscellaneous Provisions) (Scotland) Act 1968 are the corresponding Scottish enactments to section 10 and Part I of the Civil Evidence Act 1968.

(10) In the application of this section to Northern Ireland, for references to any subsection of section 5 or 6 of the Civil Evidence Act 1968 or to section 10 of that Act there shall be substituted references to the same subsection of section 2 or 3 1971 c. 36 (N.I.). of the Civil Evidence Act (Northern Ireland) 1971 or section 6 of that Act.

Furnishing of information and production of documents. **35.**—(1) The Commissioners may by regulations make provision for requiring taxable persons to notify to the Commissioners such particulars of changes in circumstances relating to those persons or any business carried on by them as appear to the Commissioners required for the purpose of keeping the register kept under this Part of this Act up to date.

(2) Every person who is concerned (in whatever capacity) in the supply of goods in the course of a business or to whom such a supply is made shall—

(a) furnish to the Commissioners, within such time and in such form as they may require, such information relating to the goods or to the supply as the Commissioners may specify ; and

(b) upon demand made by an authorised person, produce or cause to be produced any documents relating to the goods or to the supply for inspection by the authorised person and permit him to take copies of or to make extracts from them or to remove them at a reasonable time and for a reasonable period.

(3) Every person who is concerned (in whatever capacity) in the taxable supply of any services or to whom such a supply is made shall—

(a) furnish to the Commissioners, within such time and in such form as they may require, such information relating to the consideration for the supply or to the name and address of the person to whom the supply is made as the Commissioners may specify ; and

(b) upon demand made by an authorised person, produce or cause to be produced any documents relating to the consideration for inspection by the authorised person and permit him to take copies of or to make extracts from them or to remove them at a reasonable time and for a reasonable period.

(4) For the purposes of this section, the documents relating to the supply of goods, or to the consideration for the supply of services, in the course of a business shall be taken to include any profit and loss account and balance sheet relating to that business.

(5) Where any documents removed under the powers conferred by this section are lost or damaged the Commissioners shall be liable to compensate their owner for any expenses reasonably incurred by him in replacing or repairing the documents.

(6) In this section " document " and " copy " have the same meanings—

(a) in relation to England and Wales, as, by virtue of section 10 of the Civil Evidence Act 1968, they have in Part I of that Act ; 1968 c. 64.
1968 c. 70.

(b) in relation to Scotland, as, by virtue of section 17 of the Law Reform (Miscellaneous Provisions) (Scotland) Act 1968, they have in Part III of that Act ; and

(c) in relation to Northern Ireland, as, by virtue of section 6 of the Civil Evidence Act (Northern Ireland) 1971, they have in Part I of that Act. 1971 c. 36
(N.I.).

36.—(1) An authorised person, if it appears to him necessary for the protection of the revenue against mistake or fraud, may at any time take, from the goods in the possession of any person who supplies goods, such samples as the authorised person may require with a view to determining how the goods or the materials of which they are made ought to be or to have been treated for the purposes of tax. *Power to take samples.*

(2) Any sample taken under this section shall be disposed of and accounted for in such manner as the Commissioners may direct.

(3) Where a sample is taken under this section from the goods in any person's possession and is not returned to him within a reasonable time and in good condition the Commissioners shall pay him by way of compensation a sum equal to the cost of the sample to him or such larger sum as they may determine.

37.—(1) For the purpose of exercising any powers under this Part of this Act an authorised person may at any reasonable time enter premises used in connection with the carrying on of a business.

(2) Where an authorised person has reasonable cause to believe that any premises are used in connection with the supply of goods under taxable supplies and that goods to be so supplied are on those premises, he may at any reasonable time enter and inspect those premises and inspect any goods found on them.

(3) If a justice of the peace is satisfied on information on oath that there is reasonable ground for suspecting that an offence in connection with the tax is being, has been or is about to be committed on any premises or that evidence of the commission of such an offence is to be found there, he may issue a warrant in writing authorising any authorised person to enter those premises, if necessary by force, at any time within fourteen days from the time of the issue of the warrant and search them ; and any person who enters the premises under the authority of the warrant may—

(a) take with him such other persons as appear to him to be necessary ;

(b) seize and remove any documents or other things whatsoever found on the premises which he has reasonable cause to believe may be required as evidence for the purposes of proceedings in respect of such an offence ; and

(c) search or cause to be searched any person found on the premises whom he has reasonable cause to believe to have committed or be about to commit such an offence or to be in possession of any such documents or other things ;

but no woman or girl shall be searched except by a woman.

(4) In the application of this section to Scotland, the reference to a justice of the peace includes a reference to the sheriff and a magistrate.

38.—(1) If any person is knowingly concerned in, or in the taking of steps with a view to, the fraudulent evasion of tax by him or any other person, he shall be liable to a penalty of £1,000 or three times the amount of the tax, whichever is the greater, or to imprisonment for a term not exceeding two years, or to both.

(2) If any person—

    (a) with intent to deceive produces, furnishes or sends for the purposes of this Part of this Act or otherwise makes use for those purposes of any document which is false in a material particular ; or

    (b) in furnishing any information for the purposes of this Part of this Act makes any statement which he knows to be false in a material particular or recklessly makes a statement which is false in a material particular ;

he shall be liable to a penalty of £1,000 or to imprisonment for a term not exceeding two years, or to both.

(3) Where a person's conduct during any specified period must have involved the commission by him of one or more offences under the preceding provisions of this section, then, whether or not the particulars of that offence or those offences are known, he shall, by virtue of this subsection, be guilty of an offence and liable to a penalty of £1,000 or three times the amount of any tax that was or was intended to be evaded by his conduct, or to imprisonment for a term not exceeding two years, or to both.

(4) If any person acquires possession of or deals with any goods, or accepts the supply of any services, having reason to believe that tax on the supply of the goods or services or on the importation of the goods has been or will be evaded, he shall be liable to a penalty of £1,000 or three times the amount of the tax, whichever is the greater.

(5) If any person fails to comply with the requirements of Schedule 1 to this Act or supplies goods or services in contravention of section 32(2) of this Act he shall be liable to a penalty of £1,000 or, if greater, three times the amount of the tax evaded by the failure or contravention.

(6) If a person other than—

    (a) a person registered under this Part of this Act ; or

    (b) a person treated as a taxable person under regulations made under section 23(3) of this Act ; or

    (c) a person authorised to do so under regulations made under section 30(6) of this Act ; or

    (d) a person acting on behalf of the Crown ;

issues an invoice showing an amount as being tax or as being attributable to tax he shall be liable to a penalty of £1,000 or three times the amount so shown, whichever is the greater.

(7) If any person fails to comply with any requirement imposed under section 34 or 35 of this Act or any regulations or rules made under this Part of this Act, he shall be liable to a penalty of £100, together with a penalty of £10 for each day on which the failure continues.

1952 c. 44. (8) Sections 281 to 291 of the Customs and Excise Act 1952 (proceedings for offences, mitigation of penalties and certain other matters) shall apply in relation to offences under this Part of this Act (which include any act or omission in respect of which a penalty is imposed) and penalties imposed under this Part of this Act as they apply in relation to offences and penalties under the customs and excise Acts as defined in that Act ; and accordingly in section 290(2) as it applies by virtue of this subsection the reference to duty shall be construed as a reference to the tax.

39.—(1) A certificate of the Commissioners—

(a) that a person was or was not, at any date, registered under this Part of this Act ; or

(b) that any return required by or under this Part of this Act has not been made or had not been made at any date ; or

(c) that any tax shown as due in any return or assessment made in pursuance of this Part of this Act has not been paid ;

shall be sufficient evidence of that fact until the contrary is proved.

(2) A photograph of any document furnished to the Commissioners for the purposes of this Part of this Act and certified by them to be such a photograph shall be admissible in any proceedings, whether civil or criminal, to the same extent as the document itself.

(3) Any document purporting to be a certificate under subsection (1) or subsection (2) of this section shall be deemed to be such a certificate until the contrary is proved.

Appeals

40.—(1) An appeal shall lie to a value added tax tribunal constituted in accordance with Schedule 6 to this Act against the decision of the Commissioners with respect to any of the following matters : —

(a) the registration or cancellation of registration of any person under this Part of this Act ;

(b) an assessment under section 31 of this Act or the amount of such an assessment ;

(c) the tax chargeable on the supply of any goods or services or, subject to subsection (3) of this section, on the importation of any goods ;

(d) the amount of any input tax which may be deducted by a person ;

(e) the proportion of any supplies that is to be taken as consisting of taxable supplies ;

(f) any refusal to permit the value of supplies to be determined by a method described in a notice published under section 30(3) of this Act ;

(g) any refusal of an application under section 21 of this Act;

(h) any direction under paragraph 1 or paragraph 2 of Schedule 3 to this Act;

(i) the requirement of any security under section 32(2) of this Act.

(2) Where the appeal involves a question as to the amount of tax payable by any person it shall not be entertained unless the amount determined by the Commissioners as payable has been paid to or deposited with them; but so much of any such amount as is found on appeal not to be due shall be repaid with interest at such rate as the value added tax tribunal may determine.

(3) No appeal shall lie under this section with respect to any matter that has been or could have been referred to arbitration under section 260 of the Customs and Excise Act 1952 as applied by section 17 of this Act.   1952 c. 44.

Supplementary

41.—(1) There shall be included among the debts which— *Priority of tax in bankruptcy, winding-up, etc.*

(a) under section 33 of the Bankruptcy Act 1914 are to be paid in priority to all other debts in the distribution of the property of a bankrupt or person dying insolvent; or   1914 c. 59.

1913 c. 20. (b) under section 118 of the Bankruptcy (Scotland) Act 1913 are to be paid in priority to all other debts in the division of a bankrupt's estate; or

1964 c. 32. (N.I.). (c) under section 1 of the Preferential Payments (Bankruptcies and Arrangements) Act (Northern Ireland) 1964 are to be paid in priority to all other debts in the distribution of the property of a bankrupt, arranging debtor or person dying insolvent; or

1948 c. 38. 1960 c. 22. (N.I.). (d) under section 319 of the Companies Act 1948 or section 287 of the Companies Act (Northern Ireland) 1960 are to be paid in priority to all other debts in the winding up of a company, or under section 94 of the Act of 1948 or section 92 of the Act of 1960 are on an appointment of a receiver on behalf of debenture holders or taking of possession by or on behalf of debenture holders to be paid in priority to any claim for principal or interest in respect of the debentures;

the amount of any tax due at the relevant date from the bankrupt, debtor, person dying or company and having become due within the twelve months next before that date.

(2) In this section " the relevant date "—

(a) in relation to section 33 of the Act of 1914, means the date of the receiving order or of the death, as the case may be;

(*b*) in relation to section 118 of the Act of 1913, means the date mentioned in subsection (4) of that section ;

(*c*) in relation to section 1 of the Act of 1964, means the date of the order of adjudication, the date of the filing of a petition for arrangement or of the death, as the case may be ;

(*d*) in relation to section 319 of the Act of 1948, or section 287 of the Act of 1960, has the meaning assigned to it by that section, and in relation to section 94 of the Act of 1948 or section 92 of the Act of 1960, means the date of the appointment of the receiver or taking of possession ;

and for the purposes of this section the tax having become due within the twelve months mentioned therein in respect of any prescribed accounting period falling partly within and partly outside those twelve months shall be taken to be such part of the tax due for the whole of that accounting period as is proportionate to the part of that period falling within those twelve months.

42.—(1) Where, after the making of a contract for the supply of goods or services and before the goods or services are supplied, there is a change in the tax charged on the supply, then, unless the contract otherwise provided, there shall be added to or deducted from the consideration for the supply an amount equal to the change. *Adjustment of contracts on changes in tax.*

(2) References in this section to a change in the tax charged on a supply include references to a change to or from no tax being charged on the supply.

43.—(1) Any order under this Part of this Act may be varied or revoked by a subsequent order. *Orders, rules and regulations.*

(2) Any order made by the Treasury and any regulations or rules under this Part of this Act shall be made by statutory instrument.

(3) Any statutory instrument made under this Part of this Act shall be subject to annulment in pursuance of a resolution of the Commons House of Parliament, except an Order in Council and an order making such provision as is mentioned in subsection (4) of this section.

(4) An order under this Part of this Act making provision—

(*a*) for increasing the rate of tax in force at the time of the making of the order ; or

(*b*) for excepting any input tax from the provisions of subsections (1) to (5) of section 3 of this Act ; or

(*c*) for varying Schedule 4 or Schedule 5 to this Act so as to abolish the zero-rating of a supply or to abolish the exemption of a supply without zero-rating it ;

shall be laid before the Commons House of Parliament ; and

unless it is approved by that House before the expiration of a period of twenty-eight days beginning with the date on which it was made, it shall cease to have effect on the expiration of that period, but without prejudice to anything previously done thereunder or to the making of a new order.

In reckoning any such period no account shall be taken of any time during which Parliament is dissolved or prorogued or during which the Commons House of Parliament is adjourned for more than four days.

44. A notice to be served on any person for any of the purposes of this Part of this Act may be served by sending it by post in a letter addressed to that person at his last or usual residence or place of business.

Service of notices.

45.—(1) In this Part of this Act " business " includes any trade, profession or vocation ; and

Meaning of " business ", etc.

> (a) the provision by the Independent Broadcasting Authority of broadcasting services ; and
>
> (b) the provision by a club or by an association to which this paragraph applies of the facilities available to its members ; and
>
> (c) the provision by an organisation to which this paragraph applies of the advantages of membership ; and
>
> (d) the admission, for a consideration, of persons to any premises,

shall be deemed to be the carrying on of a business

(2) Paragraph (b) of the preceding subsection applies to any association providing facilities for its members but shall not be taken to apply to an organisation of workers (within the meaning of section 61 of the Industrial Relations Act 1971 as extended by section 86 of that Act) ; and paragraph (c) of that subsection applies to any organisation of persons carrying on a trade, profession or vocation and to any association of such organisations, but only if the organisation or association so elects by notice in writing given to the Commissioners.

1971 c. 72.

(3) Where a person, in the course of carrying on a trade, profession or vocation, accepts an office, other than a public office, any services supplied by him as holder of the office shall be treated for the purposes of this Part of this Act as supplied in the course of a business carried on by him.

46.—(1) In this Part of this Act—

Interpretation.

> " assignment ", in relation to Scotland, means assignation ;
>
> " authorised person " means any person acting under the authority of the Commissioners ;
>
> " invoice " includes any document similar to an invoice ;
>
> " input tax " has the meaning assigned to it by section 3 of this Act ;
>
> " money " includes currencies other than sterling ;

" prescribed accounting period " has the meaning assigned to it by section 30(1) of this Act ;

" quarter " means a period of three months ending at the end of March, June, September or December ;

" ship " includes hovercraft ;

" tax " means value added tax ;

" taxable person " has the meaning assigned to it by section 4 of this Act ;

" taxable supply " means any supply of goods or services in the United Kingdom other than an exempt supply ;

" the Commissioners " means the Commissioners of Customs and Excise.

(2) Schedules 4 and 5 to this Act shall be interpreted in accordance with the notes contained therein ; and accordingly the powers conferred by this Act to vary those Schedules include a power to add to, delete or vary those notes.

(3) The descriptions of Groups in those Schedules are for ease of reference only and shall not affect the interpretation of the descriptions of items in those Groups.

(4) References in this Part of this Act to the United Kingdom include the territorial sea of the United Kingdom.

47.—(1) Tax shall not be charged on any supply or importation taking place before 1st April 1973. Commencement.

(2) Notwithstanding anything in section 7 of this Act or in section 79 of the Customs and Excise Act 1952 as applied by section 17 of this Act— 1952 c. 44.

> (a) a payment made or invoice issued before 1st April 1973 may be disregarded in determining for the purposes of this section whether a supply takes place before that date if, or to the extent that, it appears to the Commissioners that it would not have been so made or issued but for the tax ; and
>
> (b) goods of which entry is made under section 28 of the Customs and Excise Act 1952 shall be treated for the purposes of this section as imported on the date on which entry is so made.

48. Where a vehicle in respect of which purchase tax has been remitted under section 23 of the Purchase Tax Act 1963 (vehicles acquired for use outside United Kingdom) is brought back to the United Kingdom, the vehicle shall not, when brought back, be treated as imported for the purpose of value added tax chargeable on the importation of goods. Vehicles brought back to U.K. after remission of purchase tax. 1963 c. 9.

49.—(1) If an Act of Tynwald makes provision similar to the provision made with respect to value added tax by this Act, Her Majesty may by Order in Council make provision for securing that— Isle of Man.

(a) tax is charged under either Act as if references therein to the United Kingdom or the Isle of Man included both the United Kingdom and the Isle of Man, but is not charged under both Acts in respect of the same transaction ; and

(b) persons who are taxable persons for the purposes of either Act are treated as taxable persons for the purposes also of the other ; and

(c) a removal of goods from the United Kingdom into the Isle of Man or from the Isle of Man into the United Kingdom is not treated for the purposes of either Act as an importation or exportation of the goods ;

and for making such modifications in those Acts and orders rules and regulations made thereunder as may be requisite for those purposes ; and similarly with respect to any Act passed after this Act and relating to value added tax.

(2) An Order in Council under this section may include provision for section 2 of the Isle of Man Act 1958 (Isle of Man share of certain duties) to apply as if value added tax and the tax for which provision is made by Act of Tynwald were included among the duties mentioned in subsection (4) of that section and as if the reference in subsection (2)(a) of that section to goods consumed or used in the Isle of Man included a reference to services supplied in the Island.

1958 c. 11.

Refund of tax to Government of Northern Ireland. **50.** The Commissioners shall refund to the Government of Northern Ireland the amount of the tax charged on the supply of goods or services to, or on the importation of goods by, that Government, after deducting therefrom so much of that amount as may be agreed between them and the Ministry of Finance for Northern Ireland as attributable to supplies and importations for the purpose of a business carried on by the Government of Northern Ireland.

PART II

CAR TAX AND PURCHASE TAX

Car tax. **51.**—(1) A tax, to be known as car tax, shall be charged after 31st March 1973 on all chargeable vehicles made or registered in the United Kingdom.

(2) Car tax on any vehicle shall be charged at the rate of 10 per cent. of the wholesale value of the vehicle

(3) In this section " chargeable vehicle " means, subject to the following provisions of this section, any vehicle of a kind normally used on public roads which is propelled by an internal combustion engine, has three or more wheels and either—

(a) is constructed or adapted solely or mainly for the carriage of passengers; or

(b) has to the rear of the driver's seat roofed accommodation which is fitted with side windows or which is constructed or adapted for the fitting of side windows.

(4) The following are not chargeable vehicles—

   (*a*) vehicles capable of accommodating only one person or suitable for carrying twelve or more persons;

   (*b*) vehicles of not less than three tons unladen weight;

   (*c*) caravans, ambulances and prison vans;

   (*d*) vehicles of a type approved by the Assistant Commissioner of Police of the Metropolis as conforming to the conditions of fitness for the time being laid down by him for the purposes of the London Cab Order 1934;

   (*e*) vehicles constructed for a special purpose other than the carriage of persons and having no other accommodation for carrying persons than such as is incidental to that purpose.

(5) The Treasury may by order made by statutory instrument delete or vary any description of vehicle for the time being specified in subsection (4) of this section or add a description of vehicle to those so specified; and any such order may contain such transitional provisions as appear to the Treasury to be necessary or expedient.

A statutory instrument made under this subsection shall be subject to annulment in pursuance of a resolution of the Commons House of Parliament except such an order as is mentioned in subsection (6) of this section.

(6) An order under subsection (5) of this section the effect of which is to include any description of vehicle among those which are chargeable vehicles shall be laid before the Commons House of Parliament; and unless it is approved by that House before the expiration of a period of twenty-eight days beginning with the date on which it was made it shall cease to have effect on the expiration of that period, but without prejudice to anything previously done thereunder or to the making of a new order.

In reckoning any such period no account shall be taken of any time during which Parliament is dissolved or prorogued or during which the Commons House of Parliament is adjourned for more than four days.

(7) A vehicle is not a chargeable vehicle if it is more than twenty years old.

(8) A vehicle is not a chargeable vehicle if purchase tax has been paid in respect of it.

(9) References in this section to the making of a chargeable vehicle include references to the conversion into a chargeable vehicle of a vehicle of any other description.

1971 c. 10. (10) In this section " registered " means registered under the Vehicles (Excise) Act 1971 or any corresponding enactment of the Parliament of Northern Ireland for the time being in force.

(11) Schedule 7 to this Act shall have effect in relation to the car tax.

52. Subject to any new order of the Treasury under section 2 of the Purchase Tax Act 1963, Part I of Schedule 1 to that Act (chargeable and exempt goods and rates of tax) as amended shall have effect as from 22nd March 1972 with the substitution for any reference to 45 per cent. or 30 per cent. of a reference to 25 per cent.

53.—(1) Purchase tax shall not be charged in any case where, under the provisions of the Purchase Tax Act 1963, it would become due after 31st March 1973 or where, under the enactments applied by section 25 of that Act to tax chargeable under section 11 thereof, it would be payable after that date.

(2) Subsection (1) of this section shall not affect—

(a) the operation of section 13(4) of the Purchase Tax Act 1963 (tax on imported goods not accounted for to satisfaction of Commissioners) in relation to goods deemed to be imported as mentioned in subsection (3) of that section on a representation made before April 1973 ; or

(b) any liability to tax arising on the breach of a condition subject to which relief from purchase tax was given.

(3) Where a person carries on a business before 1st April 1973 in such circumstances that he is required under section 4(1) of the Purchase Tax Act 1963 to be registered but the relevant date mentioned in section 5(1) of that Act (applications for registration) falls not earlier than fourteen days before that day, that section shall have effect as if it required him to give to the Commissioners of Customs and Excise, before the expiration of fourteen days from the relevant date, notice in writing of his so carrying on the business.

(4) Notwithstanding anything in section 14 of the Purchase Tax Act 1963, no process completed after 31st March 1973 shall be a chargeable process within the meaning of that Act.

(5) Where a person is, on 31st March 1973, under a duty to preserve records and accounts kept under section 24 of the Purchase Tax Act 1963, that duty, and his obligation to produce them for inspection, shall continue after that date, notwithstanding that he is no longer registered or required to be registered under that Act.

(6) In relation to any time falling after 31st March 1973 references to registered persons in section 31 of the Purchase Tax Act 1963 and in any regulations made under that section before the passing of this Act shall have effect as references to persons who were registered persons before 1st April 1973 ; and the reference to a registered person in section 12(3) of that Act shall be construed accordingly.

(7) Regulations under section 31 of the Purchase Tax Act 1963 may make provision for requiring persons—

(a) to keep, on and after 1st October 1972, and preserve for such period as may be specified in the regulations, records in such form and containing such particulars as may be so specified of chargeable goods in their possession in circumstances where the delivery of the goods is liable, under section 40(4) of that Act, to be treated as a delivery under a chargeable purchase, and of such purchases made of such goods, and to produce the records for inspection by any officer or other person authorised in that behalf by the Commissioners of Customs and Excise at such time and at such place as that officer or person may require ; and

(b) to furnish, at such times and places as may be specified in the regulations, to persons who have delivered such goods statements in such form and containing such particulars of goods remaining in the possession of the persons furnishing the statements and of purchases made of the goods as may be so specified, and to require such statements to contain a declaration, signed by the person to whom the goods were delivered or on his behalf by such persons as may be specified in the regulations, that the statement is to the best of his knowledge correct and complete.

(8) The enactments mentioned in Part I of Schedule 28 to this Act are hereby repealed, to the extent specified in the third column of that Part, as from the end of March 1973 ; and the enactments mentioned in Part II of that Schedule are hereby repealed, to the extent specified in the third column of that Part, as from such date as the Treasury may by order made by statutory instrument appoint, and different dates may be so appointed for different enactments.

Amendments consequential on replacement of purchase tax.
1947 c. 44.

1968 c. 44.

1961 c. 36.

54.—(1) In section 14(2) of the Crown Proceedings Act 1947 (summary applications to High Court for payment of purchase tax and furnishing of information relating thereto) and in section 14 of that Act as it applies in Northern Ireland for the words " purchase tax " in paragraphs (c) and (d) there shall be substituted the words " value added tax " ; but without prejudice to the operation of that section as originally enacted (or of the section substituted for Northern Ireland) with respect to purchase tax becoming due before the coming into force of this section or with respect to so much of the enactments relating to purchase tax as remains in force thereafter.

(2) In subsections (1) and (2) of section 7 of the Finance Act 1968 (relief from customs duty and purchase tax payable by persons entering the United Kingdom and simplified computation of duty and tax) for the words " purchase tax ", wherever they occur, there shall be substituted the words " value added tax ".

(3) For subsection (6) of that section there shall be substituted the following subsection—

" (6) In this section " value added tax " means value added tax chargeable on the importation of goods and references to customs duty include any addition thereto by virtue of section 9 of the Finance Act 1961 ".

(4) In section 6(1) of the Finance Act 1968 for the words following paragraph (a) there shall be substituted the following words—

> " (b) being dutiable goods or chargeable goods, he has obtained in the United Kingdom without payment of duty or tax ;

and in respect of which he is not entitled to exemption from duty and tax by virtue of any order under section 7 of this Act.

In this subsection ' chargeable goods ' means goods on the importation of which value added tax is chargeable or goods obtained in the United Kingdom before 1st April 1973 which are chargeable goods within the meaning of the Purchase Tax Act 1963 ; and ' tax ' means value added tax or purchase tax."

1968 c. 48.

(5) In section 9 of the International Organisations Act 1968 for the words " or of purchase tax " there shall be substituted the words " value added tax or car tax " and in paragraph 7 of Schedule 1 to that Act for the words " purchase tax paid on any goods " there shall be substituted the words " car tax paid on any vehicles and value added tax paid on the supply of any goods or services " ; but without prejudice to the operation of that section or paragraph as originally enacted with respect to purchase tax becoming due before the coming into force of this section.

1971 c. 10.

(6) In section 6 of the Vehicles (Excise) Act 1971 (exemption from vehicles excise duty of vehicles acquired by overseas residents) the following shall be substituted for subsection (1), but without prejudice to the operation of that subsection as originally enacted in relation to purchase tax remitted under section 23 of the Purchase Tax Act 1963 :

1963 c. 9.

> " (1) A mechanically propelled vehicle shall not be chargeable with any duty under this Act if it has been supplied to the person keeping it by a taxable person within the meaning of section 4 of the Finance Act 1972 and the supply has been zero-rated in pursuance of subsection (7) of section 12 of that Act ; but if, at any time, the value added tax that would have been chargeable on the supply but for the zero-rating becomes payable under subsection (8) of that section, or would have become so payable but for any authorisation or waiver under that subsection, then the provisions of subsection (3) below shall apply in relation to that vehicle ".

(7) This section shall come into force on 1st April 1973.

SCHEDULES

SCHEDULE 1

VALUE ADDED TAX—REGISTRATION

Liability to be registered

1. A person who makes taxable supplies but is not registered is liable to be registered—

    (*a*) after the end of any quarter, if the value of his taxable supplies in the period of one, two, three or four quarters then ending has exceeded the amount shown in the following Table as applicable to that period ; or

    (*b*) at any time, if there are reasonable grounds for believing that the value of his taxable supplies in the period of one year beginning at that or any later time will exceed £5,000 ;

except that a person is not liable to be registered by virtue of sub-paragraph (*a*) above on the ground that the value of his taxable supplies in a period of less than a year has exceeded the amount applicable to that period if the Commissioners are satisfied that the value of his taxable supplies in that period and the remaining quarter or quarters of the year will not exceed £5,000.

TABLE

Number of quarters comprised in period							Amount applicable £
1	...	...	...	...	...	...	1,750
2	...	...	...	...	...	...	3,000
3	...	...	...	...	...	...	4,250
4	...	...	...	...	...	...	5,000

2. A registered person who makes taxable supplies shall cease to be liable to be registered—

    (*a*) after the end of any quarter, if he has been registered for the whole of the two years then ending and the value of his taxable supplies in each of those years has been £4,000 or less, or the value of his taxable supplies in each of the quarters comprised in those years has been £1,250 or less ; and

    (*b*) at any time, if the Commissioners are satisfied that the value of his taxable supplies in the period of one year then beginning will be £4,000 or less.

Notification of liability and registration

3. A person who, on 1st April 1973, will be liable to be registered shall notify the Commissioners of that fact within ten days of the earliest date after September 1972 on which he knows or could with reasonable diligence have known that he will be so liable or within such longer time as the Commissioners may allow ; and the Commissioners shall register any such person with effect from 1st April 1973.

4. The following three paragraphs apply to persons not required to notify the Commissioners under paragraph 3 of this Schedule.

5. A person who by virtue of paragraph 1(*a*) of this Schedule is liable to be registered after the end of any quarter shall notify the Commissioners of his liability within ten days of the end of that quarter and the Commissioners shall register any such person with effect from the twenty-first day of the next quarter or such earlier date as may be agreed between them and that person.

6. A person who, by virtue of paragraph 1(b) of this Schedule, is liable to be registered by reason of the value of his taxable supplies in any period shall notify the Commissioners of that liability not later than the beginning of that period, and the Commissioners shall register any such person with effect from the beginning of that period or such earlier date as may be agreed between them and that person.

7. Where a person who intends to make taxable supplies, and will be liable to be registered when he does so, notifies the Commissioners of the fact and requests to be registered the Commissioners may, subject to such conditions as they think fit to impose, register him from such date as may be agreed between them and that person.

Notification of end of liability and cancellation of registration

8. A registered person who ceases to make taxable supplies shall notify the Commissioners of that fact within ten days of the date on which he does so and the Commissioners shall cancel the registration of any such person.

9. Where, by virtue of paragraph 2(a) of this Schedule, a registered person ceases to be liable to be registered and notifies the Commissioners of that fact, the Commissioners shall cancel his registration with effect from the end of the period of fourteen days beginning with the date on which he so notifies them or from such other date as may be agreed between them and that person.

10. Where a registered person requests the Commissioners to cancel his registration by virtue of paragraph 2(b) of this Schedule and the Commissioners are at any time satisfied as mentioned in that paragraph they shall cancel his registration as from that time.

Discretionary registration or exemption from registration

11. Notwithstanding the preceding provisions of this Schedule,—

 (a) where a person who makes or intends to make taxable supplies satisfies the Commissioners that any such supply is zero-rated or would be zero-rated if he were a taxable person they may, if he so requests and they think fit, exempt him from registration ; and

 (b) where a person who makes or intends to make taxable supplies is not and will not be liable to be registered the Commissioners may, if he so requests and they think fit, treat him as so liable, subject to such conditions as they think fit to impose ;

until it appears to the Commissioners that the request should no longer be acted upon or the request is withdrawn ; but the Commissioners may by notice given in such manner as appears to them appropriate for the information of persons making taxable supplies prevent the withdrawal of such a request made after the publication of the notice for such period after it is made as may be specified in the notice.

Supplementary

12. The provisions of this Part of this Act relating to the determination of the value of a supply of goods or services shall apply for the purposes of this Schedule with the modification that no allowance shall be made for tax.

13. Any notification required under this Schedule shall be made in such form and shall contain such particulars as the Commissioners may by regulations prescribe.

14. References in this Schedule to registration are references to registration in a register kept by the Commissioners for the purposes of this Part of this Act.

Section 5

SCHEDULE 2

MATTERS TO BE TREATED AS SUPPLY OF GOODS

1. Where goods acquired or produced by a taxable person in the course of a business carried on by him are applied by him to the personal use of himself or any other person they shall be deemed to be supplied by him in the course of that business.

2. Where goods acquired or produced by a taxable person in the course of a business carried on by him are, under any power exercisable by another person, sold by the other person in or towards satisfaction of a debt owed by the taxable person they shall be deemed to be supplied by the taxable person in the course of that business.

3. Where a person ceases to be a taxable person, any goods then forming part of the assets of a business carried on by him shall be deemed to be supplied by him in the course of that business immediately before he ceases to be a taxable person, unless—

(a) the business is transferred as a going concern to another taxable person ; or

(b) the business is carried on by another person who, under regulations made under section 23(3) of this Act, is treated as a taxable person.

SCHEDULE 3

VALUE OF SUPPLY—SPECIAL CASES

1. Where it appears to the Commissioners—

(a) that a taxable person has supplied goods or services for a consideration in money the amount of which has been determined with a view to securing a reduction of liability to tax ; and

(b) that it is likely that goods or services will be similarly supplied by him ; and

(c) that it is necessary for the protection of the revenue to exercise their powers under this paragraph ;

they may by notice in writing give directions to that person for securing that the value by reference to which tax is charged on any supply by him of goods or services after the giving of the notice or after such later date as may be specified therein is not less than the open market value of the supply.

2. Where it appears to the Commissioners—

(a) that a taxable person supplies goods under taxable supplies to a number of individuals for sale by retail ; and (*b*) that those individuals are not taxable persons ; and

     (*c*) that it is necessary for the protection of the revenue to exercise their powers under this paragraph ;

they may by notice in writing give directions to the taxable person for securing that the value by reference to which tax is charged on any such supply by him after the giving of the notice or after such later date as may be specified therein shall be determined as if the consideration given by any such individual for the supply were equal to the price at which the goods are sold by that individual.

3. Where goods are supplied in pursuance of an agreement with respect to which the requirements of section 7 of the Hire-Purchase Act 1965, section 7 of the Hire-Purchase (Scotland) Act 1965 ^{1965 c. 66.} or section 7 of the Hire-Purchase Act (Northern Ireland) 1966 ^{1965 c. 67.} are complied with the consideration for the supply shall be taken for ^{1966 c. 42 (N.I.).} the purposes of this Part of this Act to be the cash price stated in the agreement.

4. Where goods or services are supplied for a consideration in money which is to be reduced if payment is made immediately or within a specified time the consideration shall be taken for the purposes of this Part of this Act as so reduced whether or not payment is so made.

5. Where a right to receive goods or services for an amount stated on any token, stamp or voucher is granted for a consideration, the consideration shall be disregarded for the purposes of this Part of this Act except to the extent (if any) that it exceeds that amount.

6. Where a supply is a gift of goods or a supply deemed to be made under paragraph 1 of Schedule 2 to this Act, the value of the supply shall be taken to be the cost of the goods to the person making the supply ; except that if that cost does not exceed £10 and the supply is a gift its value shall be taken to be nil.

7. Where a supply of services consists in the provision of accommodation in a hotel, inn, boarding house or similar establishment for a period exceeding four weeks—

     (*a*) the value of so much of the supply as is in excess of four weeks shall be taken to be reduced to such part thereof as is attributable to facilities other than the right to occupy the accommodation ; and

     (*b*) that part shall be taken to be not less than 20 per cent.

8. A direction under paragraph 1 or paragraph 2 of this Schedule may be varied or withdrawn by the Commissioners by a further direction given by notice in writing.

Section 12.

SCHEDULE 4

ZERO-RATING

GROUP 1—FOOD

The supply of anything comprised in the general items set out below, except—

     (*a*) a supply in the course of catering ; and

     (*b*) a supply of anything comprised in the excepted items set out below, unless it is also comprised in the items overriding the exceptions set out below.

General items

Item No.

1. Food of a kind used for human consumption.

2. Animal feeding stuffs.

3. Seeds or other means of propagation of plants comprised in item 1 or 2.

4. Live animals of a kind generally used as, or yielding or producing, food for human consumption.

Excepted items

Item No.

1. Ice cream, ice lollies, frozen yoghurt, water ices and similar frozen products, and prepared mixes and powders for making such products.

2. Chocolates, sweets and similar confectionery (including drained, glacé or crystallized fruits); and chocolate biscuits and other confectionery having a case or coating of chocolate couverture, but not including cakes in such a case or coating.

3. Beverages chargeable with any duty of customs or excise specifically charged on spirits, beer, wine or British wine and other manufactured beverages, including fruit juices and bottled waters, and syrups, concentrates, essences, powders, crystals or other products for the preparation of beverages.

4. Any of the following when packaged for human consumption without further preparation, namely, potato crisps, potato sticks, potato puffs and similar products made from the potato, or from potato flour, or from potato starch, and savoury food products obtained by the swelling of cereals or cereal products; and salted or roasted nuts other than nuts in shell.

5. Pet foods, canned, packaged or prepared; packaged foods (not being pet foods) for birds other than poultry or game; and biscuits and meal for cats and dogs.

Items overriding the exceptions

Item No.

1. Chocolate couverture not prepared or put up for retail sale.

2. Drained cherries.

3. Candied peels.

4. Tea, maté, herbal teas and similar products, and preparations and extracts thereof.

5. Cocoa, coffee and chicory and other roasted coffee substitutes, and preparations and extracts thereof.

6. Preparations and extracts of meat, yeast, egg or milk.

Notes :

(1) " Food " includes drink.

(2) " Animal " includes bird, fish, crustacean and mollusc.

(3) A supply of anything in the course of catering includes any supply of it for consumption on the premises on which it is supplied.

Item No.

1. Water other than—
   (a) distilled water ; and
   (b) water comprised in the excepted items set out in Group 1.

GROUP 3—BOOKS, ETC.

Item No.

1. Books, booklets, brochures, pamphlets and leaflets.
2. Newspapers, journals and periodicals.
3. Children's picture books and painting books.
4. Music (printed, duplicated or manuscript).
5. Maps, charts and topographical plans.
6. Covers, cases and other articles supplied with items 1 to 5 and not separately accounted for.

Note : This Group does not include plans or drawings for industrial, architectural, engineering, commercial or similar purposes.

GROUP 4—NEWSPAPER ADVERTISEMENTS

Item No.

1. The publication in any newspaper, journal or periodical of any advertisement.
2. The preparation of any advertisement intended for publication solely or mainly in one or more newspapers, journals or periodicals.
3. The supply of services for the purpose of securing such a publication or a preparation as is mentioned in item 1 or 2.

GROUP 5—NEWS SERVICES

Item No.

1. The supply to newspapers or to the public of information of a kind published in newspapers.

Note : This item does not include the supply of photographs.

GROUP 6—FUEL AND POWER

Item No.

1. Coal, coke and other solid mineral fuels.
2. Coal gas, water gas, producer gases and similar gases.
3. Petroleum gases and other gaseous hydrocarbons, whether in a gaseous or liquid state.
4. Hydrocarbon oil, petrol substitutes and power methylated spirits (within the meaning of the Hydrocarbon Oil (Customs and Excise) Act 1971).
5. Electricity, heat and air-conditioning.

GROUP 7—CONSTRUCTION OF BUILDINGS, ETC.

Item No.

1. The granting, by a person constructing a building, of a major interest in, or in any part of, the building or its site.

2. The supply, in the course of the construction, alteration or demolition of any building or of any civil engineering work, of any services other than the services of an architect, surveyor or any person acting as consultant or in a supervisory capacity.

3. The supply, in connection with a supply of services falling within item 2, of materials or of builder's hardware, sanitary ware or other articles of a kind ordinarily installed by builders as fixtures.

Notes:

(1) Item 2 does not include any work of repair or maintenance or the supply of any services to a person who himself supplies such services as are mentioned therein.

(2) " Major interest " has the same meaning as in section 5(6) of this Act.

(3) Section 12(3) of this Act does not apply to goods forming part of a description of supply in this Group.

GROUP 8—SERVICES TO OVERSEAS TRADERS OR FOR OVERSEAS PURPOSES

Item No.

1. Any services supplied by an agent to his principal if the principal is an overseas trader.

2. The application of any treatment or process to goods imported on behalf of an overseas trader for subsequent re-export and in fact re-exported.

3. The preparation, publication or dissemination of any advertisement on behalf of an overseas trader.

4. The supply of any services for the purpose of securing the preparation, publication or dissemination of any advertisement on behalf of an overseas trader.

5. The supply to an overseas trader or an overseas authority, in such circumstances as may be specified by order of the Treasury, of such services comprised in Group 2 or Group 5 of Schedule 5 to this Act as may be so specified.

6. The supply to an overseas trader of any services not used in the United Kingdom and not included in items 1 to 5 of this Group nor in any Group in Schedule 5 to this Act.

7. The supply to an overseas authority of any services not comprised in item 5 of this Group nor in any Group in Schedule 5 to this Act.

8. The preparation of plans and specifications for construction operations outside the United Kingdom.

9. The granting, assignment or surrender of any right exercisable outside the United Kingdom.

Notes:

(1) For the purposes of this Group a person is an overseas trader if he carries on a business outside the United Kingdom, and—

(*a*) does not carry on a business in the United Kingdom ; and

(*b*) is neither resident nor (if a company) incorporated in the United Kingdom.

(2) Overseas authority means any State other than the United Kingdom or any part of or place in such a State or the Government of any such State, part or place.

(3) Items 3 and 4 do not apply where the overseas trader is an agent or subsidiary of any person who carries on a business in the United Kingdom or who is resident or incorporated in the United Kingdom.

(4) Items 5 and 7 do not include the supply of any services to any agency or establishment in the United Kingdom.

Group 9—Transport

Item No.

1. The supply, repair or maintenance of any ship which is neither—
    (a) a ship of a gross tonnage of less than 15 tons ; nor
    (b) a ship designed or adapted for use for recreation or pleasure.

2. The supply, repair or maintenance of any aircraft which is neither—
    (a) an aircraft of a weight of less than eighteen thousand pounds ; nor
    (b) an aircraft designed or adapted for use for recreation or pleasure.

3. Transport of passengers—
    (a) in any vehicle, ship or aircraft designed or adapted to carry not less than twelve passengers ; or
    (b) by the Post Office ; or
    (c) on any scheduled flight.

4. Transport of passengers or freight outside the United Kingdom or to or from a place outside the United Kingdom.

5. Any services provided for the handling of ships or aircraft in a port or customs airport or for the handling, in a port or customs airport, of goods carried in a ship or aircraft.

6. Pilotage services.

7. Salvage or towage services.

8. Any services supplied within or outside the United Kingdom for or in connection with the surveying of any ship or aircraft or the classification of any ship or aircraft for the purposes of any register.

9. The making of arrangements for the supply of, or of space in, any ship or aircraft or for the supply of any service included in items 1 to 8.

Note : " Port " and " customs airport " have the same meanings as in the Customs and Excise Act 1952.

1952 c. 44.

Group 10—Caravans

Item No.

1. Caravans exceeding the limits of size for the time being permitted for the use of trailers on roads.

Note: This item does not include removable contents other than goods of a kind mentioned in Item 3 of Group 7.

Group 11—Gold

Item No.

1. The supply of any gold bullion.

2. The supply of gold coins by an authorised dealer in gold to another such dealer.

Notes:
(1) " Authorised dealer in gold " means a person for the time being authorised by an order of the Treasury under the Exchange Control Act 1947 to act for the purposes of that Act as an authorised dealer 1947 c. 14. in relation to gold ; and " gold bullion " means any newly mined gold and refined bar gold or gold grain of not less than 995 millesimal fineness.

(2) Section 12(3) of this Act does not apply to gold coins.

GROUP 12—BANK NOTES

Item No.
1. The issue by a bank of a note payable to bearer on demand.

GROUP 13—DRUGS, MEDICINES AND APPLIANCES SUPPLIED ON PRESCRIPTION

Item No.
1. The supply of any goods dispensed, by a person registered in the register of pharmaceutical chemists kept under the Pharmacy Act 1954 or the Pharmacy and Poisons Act 1954 c. 61. (Northern Ireland) 1925, on the prescription of a person 1925 c. 8 (N.I.). registered in the register of medical practitioners, the register of temporarily registered medical practitioners or the dentists' register.

Note: Section 12(3) of this Act does not apply to goods forming part of this description of supply.

SCHEDULE 5   Section 13.
EXEMPTIONS
GROUP 1—LAND

Item No.
1. The grant, assignment or surrender of any interest in or right over land or of any licence to occupy land, other than—
    (a) the provision of accommodation in a hotel, inn, boarding house or similar establishment or in a house, flat or caravan used wholly or mainly for the provision of holiday accommodation ;
    (b) the granting of facilities for camping in tents or caravans ;
    (c) the granting of facilities for parking a vehicle ; and
    (d) the granting of any right to take game or fish.

GROUP 2—INSURANCE

Item No.
1. The provision of insurance of any description.
2. The making of arrangements for the provision of any insurance.

GROUP 3—POSTAL SERVICES

Item No.
1. The conveyance of postal packets by the Post Office.
2. The supply by the Post Office of any services in connection with the conveyance of postal packets.

1953 c. 36.   *Note :* " Postal packet " has the same meaning as in the Post Office Act 1953, except that it does not include a telegram.

GROUP 4—BETTING, GAMING AND LOTTERIES

Item No.

1. The provision of any facilities for the placing of bets or the playing of any games of chance.

2. The granting of a right to take part in a lottery.

Notes:

(1) Item 1 does not include—

   (a) admission to any premises ; or

   (b) the granting of a right to take part in a game in respect of which a charge may be made by virtue of regulations under section 14 of the Gaming Act 1968 ; or

   (c) the provision by a club of such facilities to its members as are available to them on payment of their subscription but without further charge.

1968 c. 65. (2) " Game of chance " has the same meaning as in the Gaming Act 1968.

1971 c. 57. (3) " Lottery " includes any competition for prizes which is authorised by a licence under the Pool Competitions Act 1971.

GROUP 5—FINANCE

Item No.

1. The issue, transfer or receipt of, or any dealing with, money, any security for money or any note or order for the payment of money.

2. The making of any advance or the granting of any credit.

3. The making of arrangements for any transaction comprised in item 1 or 2.

4. The issue, transfer or receipt of, or any dealing with, any security within the definition in section 42 of the Exchange 1947 c. 14. Control Act 1947.

5. The operation of any current, deposit or savings account.

GROUP 6—EDUCATION

Item No.

1. The provision of education if—

   (a) it is provided by a school or university ; or

   (b) it is of a kind provided by a school or university and is provided otherwise than for profit.

2. The supply of any goods or services incidental to the provision of any education included in item 1.

3. The provision of any instruction supplemental to the provision of any education included in item 1.

4. The provision by a youth club of the facilities available to its members.

Notes :

(1) " School " means any institution providing primary or secondary education or both within the meaning of the Education Acts 1944 to 1971, the Education (Scotland) Acts 1939 to 1971 or the Education Acts (Northern Ireland) 1947 to 1971.

(2) " Education " includes training in any form of art.

(3) " University " includes a university college and the college, school or hall of a university.

189

Item No.

1. The supply of services and, in connection with it, the supply of goods, by a person registered or enrolled in any of the following: —

    (*a*) the register of medical practitioners or the register of temporarily registered medical practitioners ;

    (*b*) the dentists' register ;

    (*c*) either of the registers of ophthalmic opticians or the register of dispensing opticians kept under the Opticians Act 1958 or either of the lists kept 1958 c. 32. under section 4 of that Act of bodies corporate carrying on business as ophthalmic opticians or as dispensing opticians ;

    (*d*) any register kept under the Professions Supplementary to Medicine Act 1960 ; 1960 c. 66.

    (*e*) the register of nurses or the roll of nurses maintained in pursuance of section 2(1) of the Nurses 1957 c. 15. Act 1957 or kept under section 2 or section 3 of the Nurses (Scotland) Act 1951 or section 17(1) 1951 c. 55. of the Nurses and Midwives Act (Northern Ire- 1970 c. 11 (N.I.). land) 1970 ;

1951 c. 53.
1951 c. 54.
1970 c. 11 (N.I.).

    (*f*) the roll of certified midwives kept under section 2 of the Midwives Act 1951, section 3 of the Midwives (Scotland) Act 1951 or section 17(1) of the Nurses and Midwives Act (Northern Ireland) 1970 ;

1957 c. 28.

    (*g*) any roll of ancillary dental workers established under section 41 of the Dentists Act 1957.

2. The supply of any goods or services by a dental technician.

3. The supply of any services by a person registered in the register of pharmaceutical chemists kept under the Pharmacy Act 1954 or the Pharmacy and Poisons Act (Northern Ireland) 1925.

1954 c. 61.
1925 c. 8 (N.I.).

4. The provision of care or medical or surgical treatment and, in connection with it, the supply of any goods, in any hospital or other institution approved, licensed, registered or exempted from registration by any Minister or other authority.

GROUP 8—BURIAL AND CREMATION

Item No.

1. The disposal of the remains of the dead.

2. The making of arrangements for or in connection with the disposal of the remains of the dead.

Section 40

SCHEDULE 6

CONSTITUTION AND PROCEDURE OF VALUE ADDED TAX TRIBUNALS

Establishment of Value Added Tax Tribunals

1. Value added tax tribunals shall be established for England and Wales, Scotland and Northern Ireland respectively.

The President

2.—(1) There shall be a President of Value Added Tax Tribunals, who shall perform the functions conferred on him by the following provisions of this Schedule in relation to value added tax tribunals in any part of the United Kingdom.

(2) The President shall be appointed by the Lord Chancellor and shall be a barrister, advocate or solicitor of not less than ten years' standing.

3.—(1) The President may resign his office at any time and shall vacate his office at the end of the completed year of service in which he attains the age of seventy-two.

(2) The Lord Chancellor may, if he thinks fit, remove the President from office on the ground of incapacity or misbehaviour.

(3) The functions of the President may, if he is for any reason unable to act or his office is vacant, be discharged by a person nominated for the purpose by the Lord Chancellor.

(4) There shall be paid to the President such salary or fees and there may be paid to or in respect of a former President such pension, as the Treasury may with the approval of the Minister for the Civil Service determine.

Sittings of tribunals

4. Such number of value added tax tribunals shall be established as the President may from time to time with the consent of the Treasury determine, and they shall sit at such times and at such places as he may from time to time determine.

Composition of tribunals

5.—(1) A value added tax tribunal shall consist of a chairman sitting either with two other members or with one other member or alone.

(2) If the tribunal does not consist of the chairman sitting alone its decisions may be taken by a majority of votes and the chairman, if sitting with one other member, shall have a casting vote.

Membership of tribunals

6. For each sitting of a value added tax tribunal the chairman shall be either the President or a person selected by him from a panel constituted in accordance with paragraph 7 of this Schedule ; and any other member shall be a person so selected.

7.—(1) There shall be a panel of chairmen and a panel of other members of value added tax tribunals for England and Wales, Scotland and Northern Ireland respectively.

(2) Each panel of chairmen shall include one or more full-time chairmen, including one to be known as Vice-President of Value Added Tax Tribunals.

(3) A member of a panel appointed as full-time chairman shall be appointed—

(a) for England and Wales, by the Lord Chancellor ;

(b) for Scotland, by the Lord President of the Court of Session ; and

(c) for Northern Ireland, by the Lord Chief Justice of Northern Ireland ;

and all other members of a panel shall be appointed by the Treasury.

(4) There shall be paid to a full-time chairman of value added tax tribunals such salary or fees, and to other members such fees, as the Treasury, with the approval of the Minister for the Civil Service, may determine ; and the Treasury may pay to or in respect

of a former full-time chairman of value added tax tribunals such pension as they may, with that approval, determine.

Disqualifications for membership of House of Commons and exemption from jury service

8. In Part II of Schedule 1 to the House of Commons Disqualification Act 1957 (bodies of which all members are disqualified for membership) and in that part as it applies by virtue of Schedule 3 to that Act in relation to the Senate and House of Commons of Northern Ireland, there shall be inserted at the appropriate place the words " A value added tax tribunal ". 1957 c. 20.

9. No member of a value added tax tribunal shall be compelled to serve on any jury.

Rules of procedure

10. The Commissioners may make rules with respect to the procedure to be followed on appeals to value added tax tribunals and such rules may include provisions—

(*a*) for limiting the time within which appeals may be brought;

(*b*) for enabling hearings to be held in private in such circumstances as may be determined by or under the rules ;

(*c*) for parties to proceedings to be represented by such persons as may be determined by or under the rules ;

(*d*) for requiring persons to attend to give evidence and produce documents ;

(*e*) for the payment of expenses and allowances to persons attending as witnesses ;

(*f*) for the award and recovery of costs ; and

(*g*) for authorising the administration of oaths to witnesses.

Section 51.

SCHEDULE 7

Car Tax

Interpretation

1. In this Schedule " authorised person " means any person acting under the authority of the Commissioners, " the Commissioners " means the Commissioners of Customs and Excise, " the tax " means car tax and " chargeable vehicle " and (in relation to vehicles) " registered " have the same meanings as in section 51 of this Act; and references to the making of a chargeable vehicle shall be construed as in that section.

Administration and collection of tax

2.—(1) The tax shall be under the care and management of the Commissioners, who may do all such acts as may be deemed necessary and expedient for raising, collecting, receiving and accounting for the tax in like manner as they are authorised to do with relation to any duties under their care and management.

(2) All money and securities for money collected or received for or on account of the tax shall—

(*a*) if collected or received in Great Britain, be placed to the general account of the Commissioners kept at the Bank of England under section 11 of the Customs and Excise Act
1952 c. 44. 1952;

(b) if collected or received in Northern Ireland, be paid into the Consolidated Fund of the United Kingdom in such manner as the Treasury may direct.

(3) The Government of Ireland Act 1920 shall have effect as if the tax were one of the taxes mentioned in section 22(1) of that Act (reserved taxes).

(4) The Provisional Collection of Taxes Act 1968 shall be amended by inserting in subsection (1) of section 1, after the words " value added tax " the words " car tax "; and the Act as so amended shall apply in relation to a resolution of the House of Commons passed before 1st April 1974 and providing for any variation of the tax as it applies in relation to such a resolution as is mentioned in subsection (2)(a) of that section.

Liability to and payment of tax

3. Subject to paragraph 6 of this Schedule, the tax on any vehicle shall be payable—
    (a) if the vehicle is made or imported by a person registered under this Schedule, by that person ; and
    (b) in any other case by the person who for the purposes of the registration of the vehicle is treated as the person keeping the vehicle.

4.—(1) Where tax on a vehicle is payable by a person registered under this Schedule, it shall become due—
    (a) if the vehicle is appropriated to the use of that person, at the time when it is so appropriated;
    (b) if it is delivered under an agreement providing for its sale or return, at the time when, in accordance with the agreement, it ceases to be the property of that person or when it is treated for the purposes of the tax as so ceasing to be his property in pursuance of regulations made under this Schedule;
    (c) in any other case, when it is sent out from the premises of that person;
and shall become payable at the time provided for by those regulations.

(2) For the purposes of this paragraph, a vehicle which is to be sold by retail by a person registered under this Schedule shall be deemed to be sent out from the premises of that person when it is sent to the place from which it is to be sold.

5. Where tax on a vehicle is payable as mentioned in paragraph 3(b) of this Schedule it shall become due and payable before the vehicle is registered.

6.—(1) Where a chargeable vehicle is made by the conversion of a vehicle which is not a chargeable vehicle and the person converting it is not registered under this Schedule, the tax on the vehicle shall become due—
    (a) at the time the conversion is completed; or
    (b) at the time when the vehicle is first used after the conversion was begun;
whichever is the earlier, and shall be payable by the person who is the owner of the vehicle at the time the tax becomes due; except that if at that time a person other than the owner is entitled to possession of the vehicle under a hire-purchase agreement the tax shall be payable by that person instead of by the owner.

(2) Where another person carries out the conversion under a contract

to the order of the person by whom the tax is payable he shall be accountable for the tax as well as that person but may recover from him any tax paid in pursuance of this sub-paragraph.

Relief for vehicles exported

7. Tax shall not be charged on any vehicle which is shown to the satisfaction of the Commissioners to have been exported and not to have been registered before it was exported or which is to be exported under arrangements approved by the Commissioners and is not registered.

Remission of tax on vehicles acquired for export

8.—(1) Where it is shown to the satisfaction of the Commissioners that a person who acquires a chargeable vehicle is only temporarily in the United Kingdom or is about to become resident outside the United Kingdom the Commissioners may, subject to such conditions as they think necessary for the protection of the revenue, remit the tax on the vehicle.

(2) If tax has been remitted on a vehicle under sub-paragraph (1) of this paragraph and—

  (a) the vehicle is found in the United Kingdom after the date by which the Commissioners on granting the remission directed that it should be exported; or

  (b) any other condition imposed by the Commissioners under that sub-paragraph is not complied with;

and the presence of the vehicle in the United Kingdom after that date or the non-observance of that condition has not been authorised for the purposes of this sub-paragraph by the Commissioners, the tax which would have been payable but for the remission shall become payable forthwith by the person by whom the vehicle was acquired or by any other person in whose possession the vehicle is found in the United Kingdom, and shall be recoverable as a debt due to the Crown, unless, or except to the extent that, the Commissioners see fit to waive payment of the whole or part thereof.

Remission of tax on vehicles used outside United Kingdom

9.—(1) Where it is shown to the satisfaction of the Commissioners that a person who owns a chargeable vehicle has used it outside the United Kingdom for not less than such period as may be prescribed by regulations made under this Schedule they may, subject to such conditions as they think necessary for the protection of the revenue (which may include conditions prohibiting or restricting the disposal of the vehicle for a period so prescribed) remit the tax on the vehicle.

(2) If tax has been remitted on a vehicle under sub-paragraph (1) of this paragraph and any condition imposed by the Commissioners under that sub-paragraph is not complied with, the tax which would have been payable but for the remission shall be payable forthwith by the person who then owns the vehicle or by any other person in whose possession the vehicle is found, and shall be recoverable as a debt due to the Crown, unless, or except to the extent that, the Commissioners see fit to waive payment of the whole or part thereof.

Remission of tax on chargeable vehicles converted into other vehicles

10. Where it is shown to the satisfaction of the Commissioners that, under arrangements approved by them, an unused vehicle which was a chargeable vehicle has been converted into a vehicle which is not a chargeable vehicle, they may, subject to such conditions as they

think necessary for the protection of the revenue, remit the tax on the vehicle.

Wholesale value

11.—(1) For the purposes of the tax the wholesale value of any vehicle shall be taken, subject to paragraph 13(2) of this Schedule, to be the price which, in the opinion of the Commissioners, the vehicle would fetch on a sale made at the time the tax becomes due by a person selling by wholesale in the open market in the United Kingdom to a retail trader carrying on business in the United Kingdom only, on the assumption that—

(a) the price was the sole consideration for the sale; and

(b) the vehicle was to be delivered to the retail trader at the seller's place of business; and

(c) neither the tax nor value added tax was payable.

(2) In this paragraph " retail trader " means a person who sells by retail and does not sell to a person who carries on a business of selling vehicles.

Disputes as to wholesale value

12.—(1) Where the person by whom the tax is payable is dissatisfied with the determination of the wholesale value by the Commissioners he may, within such period from the time when their decision is communicated to him as may be prescribed by regulations under this Schedule or such further time as the Commissioners may allow, by notice in writing given to the Commissioners require the determination to be referred to the arbitration of a person appointed under this paragraph, whose decision shall be final and conclusive; but no such reference shall be made unless, within that period or such further time as the Commissioners may allow, the person requiring the reference has deposited with the Commissioners the amount of tax which would be due on the basis of their determination.

(2) If the tax chargeable as a result of a reference under this paragraph is less than the amount deposited with the Commissioners the excess shall be repaid with interest at such rate as the referee may determine.

(3) A referee for the purposes of this paragraph shall be appointed by the Lord Chancellor except that—

(a) if the person by whom the tax is payable has his principal place of business in Scotland, the referee shall be appointed by the Lord President of the Court of Session; and

(b) if that person has his principal place of business in Northern Ireland, the referee shall be appointed by the Lord Chief Justice of Northern Ireland.

Unfinished vehicles

13.—(1) For the purposes of the tax a vehicle which is not finished and complete but which, if finished and complete, would be a chargeable vehicle shall be treated as a chargeable vehicle.

(2) If in the opinion of the Commissioners a vehicle is not finished and complete, they shall determine its wholesale value as if it were finished and complete, having regard to the parts and accessories that remain to be provided and the processes that remain to be undergone for the vehicle to be in a state to be expected of a finished and complete chargeable vehicle.

Converted and adapted vehicles

14. Where it appears to the Commissioners that a person adapts or converts unused chargeable vehicles and that the vehicles as so adapted

195

or converted remain chargeable vehicles they may direct—

    (*a*) that the conversion or adaptation shall for the purposes of the tax be treated as the making of the vehicles resulting from it, whether or not it would otherwise fall to be so treated; and

    (*b*) that, subject to such conditions as they think necessary for the protection of the revenue, tax shall not be charged on vehicles delivered to that person, under arrangements approved by the Commissioners, by a person registered under this Schedule;

and where they so direct that person shall, while the direction is in force, be liable to be registered under this Schedule, whether or not he would otherwise be so liable.

Registration of makers and importers of chargeable vehicles

15.—(1) A person who, in any calendar year, makes or imports not less than ten chargeable vehicles is liable to be registered by the Commissioners.

(2) Every person who, on or after 1st October 1972, is liable to be registered under this paragraph and is not for the time being so registered shall notify the Commissioners of the fact within fourteen days of that date or of becoming so liable, whichever is the later; and the Commissioners may, if they think fit, register any such person.

(3) A person for the time being registered under this paragraph who ceases to make or import chargeable vehicles shall notify the Commissioners of that fact and the Commissioners shall cancel the registration of any such person when all tax due from him has been accounted for; and they may, if they think fit, cancel the registration of any other person.

(4) The Treasury may from time to time by order made by statutory instrument substitute another number for that specified in sub-paragraph (1) of this paragraph.

A statutory instrument made by virtue of this sub-paragraph shall be subject to annulment in pursuance of a resolution of the Commons House of Parliament.

Recovery of tax

16.—(1) The tax due from any person shall be recoverable as a debt due to the Crown.

(2) Regulations under this Schedule may make provision for authorising distress to be levied on the goods and chattels of any person refusing or neglecting to pay any tax due from him, and for the disposal of any goods or chattels on which distress is levied in pursuance of the regulations.

(3) In the application of the preceding sub-paragraph to Scotland, for the references to the levying of distress on any goods or chattels there shall be substituted references to the doing of diligence on goods and corporeal movables.

Power of Commissioners to assess tax due

17.—(1) Where an amount is due from any person on account of the tax, but by reason of his failure to keep or to produce or furnish any records, accounts or other documents as required by or under this Schedule, or of his failure to take or permit to be taken any other step so required, or by reason of such records, accounts or other documents being materially incomplete or inaccurate, the Commissioners are unable to ascertain the exact amount of tax due from him, the Commissioners may assess the amount due from him to the best of their judgment and notify it to him.

(2) An assessment under this paragraph of an amount of tax due shall not be made after the later of the following:—

(a) two years after the time when the amount became payable; or

(b) one year after evidence of facts, sufficient in the opinion of the Commissioners to justify the making of the assessment, comes to their knowledge;

but may, where further such evidence comes to their knowledge after the making of such an assessment, be made in addition to that assessment; but no such assessment shall be made more than six years after the time when the tax became payable, except for the purpose of recovering tax lost to the Crown through the fraud or wilful default or neglect of any person.

(3) An amount assessed and notified under this paragraph shall be recoverable as an amount of tax due unless in any action relating thereto the person liable proves the amount actually due and that amount is less than the amount assessed.

Priority of tax in bankruptcy, winding-up, etc.

18.—(1) There shall be included among the debts which—

1914 c. 59.

(a) under section 33 of the Bankruptcy Act 1914 are to be paid in priority to all other debts in the distribution of the property of a bankrupt or person dying insolvent; or

1913 c. 20.

(b) under section 118 of the Bankruptcy (Scotland) Act 1913 are to be paid in priority to all other debts in the division of a bankrupt's estate; or

1964 c. 32. (N.I.)

(c) under section 1 of the Preferential Payments (Bankruptcies and Arrangements) Act (Northern Ireland) 1964 are to be paid in priority to all other debts in the distribution of the property of a bankrupt, arranging debtor or person dying insolvent; or

1948 c. 38. 1960 c. 22. (N.I.)

(d) under section 319 of the Companies Act 1948 or section 287 of the Companies Act (Northern Ireland) 1960 are to be paid in priority to all other debts in the winding up of a company, or under section 94 of the Act of 1948 or section 92 of the Act of 1960 are on an appointment of a receiver on behalf of debenture holders or taking of possession by or on behalf of debenture holders to be paid in priority to any claim for principal or interest in respect of the debenture;

the amount of any tax due at the relevant date from the bankrupt, debtor, person dying or company and having become due within twelve months next before that date.

(2) In this paragraph " the relevant date "—

(a) in relation to section 33 of the Act of 1914 means the date of the receiving order or of the death, as the case may be;

(b) in relation to section 118 of the Act of 1913, means the date mentioned in subsection (4) of that section;

(c) in relation to section 1 of the Act of 1964 means the date of the order of adjudication, the date of the filing of a petition for arrangement or of the death as the case may be; and

(d) in relation to section 319 of the Act of 1948, or section 287 of the Act of 1960, has the meaning assigned to it by that section, and in relation to section 94 of the Act of 1948 or section 92 of the Act of 1960, means the date of the appointment of the receiver or taking of possession.

Records, accounts and returns

19.—(1) A person registered under this Schedule shall—

(a) keep such records and accounts and preserve them for such period as may be prescribed by regulations under this Schedule or as the Commissioners may direct either generally or in any particular case;

(b) if so required by or on behalf of the Commissioners, produce, at a time and place specified in the requirement, such records or accounts relating to the chargeable vehicles made or imported by him as may be so specified; and

(c) make such returns of the chargeable vehicles made or imported by him and of the amounts of tax for which he is accountable as may be prescribed by regulations under this Schedule.

(2) A person who, in the course of a business carried on by him, has chargeable vehicles delivered to him on which tax has not been paid shall—

(a) keep such records and preserve them for such periods as may be prescribed by regulations under this Schedule or as the Commissioners may direct either generally or in any particular case;

(b) if so required by or on behalf of the Commissioners, produce, at a time and place specified in the requirement, such records relating to the vehicles as may be so specified; and

(c) make to the persons by whom the vehicles are sent such returns of the vehicles ceasing or treated as ceasing to be that person's property as may be prescribed by regulations under this Schedule.

20.—(1) Every person who is concerned (in whatever capacity) with the making, sale, importation or exportation of chargeable vehicles shall—

(a) furnish to the Commissioners, within such time and in such form as they may require, such information relating to the vehicles or any materials used or kept for use in making such vehicles as the Commissioners may specify; and

(b) upon demand made by an authorised person produce or cause to be produced any documents relating to the vehicles or any materials used or kept for use in making such vehicles for inspection by the authorised person and shall permit him to take copies of or to make extracts from the documents and for that purpose to remove them at a reasonable time and for a reasonable period.

(2) Every person who converts a vehicle of another description into a chargeable vehicle shall inform the Commissioners of that fact forthwith unless he is a person registered under this Schedule.

21.—(1) An authorised person may at any reasonable time enter premises which are used in connection with the making, sale, importation or exportation of chargeable vehicles.

(2) Where an authorised person has reasonable cause to believe that any premises are used in connection with—

(a) the making, sale, importation or exportation of chargeable vehicles; or

(b) the storage of chargeable vehicles on which tax has not been paid;

and that chargeable vehicles are on those premises, he may at any reasonable time enter and inspect those premises and inspect and take account of any vehicles or materials found on them.

(3) If a justice of the peace is satisfied on information on oath that there is reasonable ground for suspecting that an offence in connection with the tax is being, has been, or is about to be committed on any premises, or that evidence of the commission of such an offence is to be found there, he may issue a warrant in writing authorising any authorised person to enter those premises, if necessary by force, at any time within fourteen days from the time of the issue of the warrant and search them; and any person who enters the premises under the authority of the warrant may—

(a) take with him such other persons as appear to him to be necessary;

(b) seize and remove any documents or other things whatsoever found on the premises which he has reasonable cause to believe may be required as evidence for the purposes of proceedings in respect of such an offence; and

(c) search or cause to be searched any person found on the premises whom he has reasonable cause to believe to have committed or to be about to commit such an offence or to be in possession of any such documents or other things;

but no woman or girl shall be searched except by a woman.

(4) In the application of sub-paragraph (3) above to Scotland, the reference to a justice of the peace includes a reference to the sheriff and a magistrate.

Offences

22.—(1) If any person is knowingly concerned in, or in the taking of steps with a view to, the fraudulent evasion of the tax by him or any other person, he shall be liable to a penalty of £1,000 or three times the amount of the tax, whichever is the greater, or to imprisonment for a term not exceeding two years, or to both.

(2) If any person—

(a) with intent to deceive produces, furnishes or sends for the purposes of this Schedule or regulations made under it or made by virtue of paragraph 27 of this Schedule, or otherwise makes use for those purposes of any document which is false in a material particular; or

(b) in furnishing any information for the purposes of this Schedule or regulations made under it makes any statement which he knows to be false in a material particular or recklessly makes a statement which is false in a material particular; or

(c) with intent to deceive uses or allows to be used any certificate issued in pursuance of regulations under this Schedule;

he shall be liable to a penalty of £1,000 or to imprisonment for a term not exceeding two years, or to both.

(3) If any person acquires possession of, deals with or uses a chargeable vehicle having reason to believe—

(a) that tax on the vehicle has been or will be evaded; or

(b) that the vehicle ought to have been registered but that tax on it has not been paid;

he shall be liable to a penalty of £1,000 or three times the amount of the tax, whichever is the greater.

(4) If a person fails to comply with any requirement imposed by or under this Schedule or regulations made under it, he shall be liable to a penalty of £100 together with a penalty of £10 for each day on which the failure continues.

(5) Sections 281 to 291 of the Customs and Excise Act 1952 (proceedings for offences, mitigation of penalties and certain other matters) shall apply in relation to offences under this paragraph (which include any act or omission in respect of which a penalty is imposed) and penalties imposed under this Schedule as they apply in relation to offences and penalties under the customs and excise Acts as defined in that Act.

1952 c. 44.

(6) Section 290(2) of the Customs and Excise Act 1952 as it applies by virtue of this paragraph shall have effect as if the question mentioned in paragraph (a) thereof were the question whether or not tax on any vehicle has become due or has been paid or secured.

Forfeiture

23. A chargeable vehicle shall be liable to forfeiture under the Customs and Excise Act 1952 if—

1952 c. 44.

    (a) tax on it would have become payable before its registration and it ought to have been but has not been registered; or

    (b) tax on it ought to have been, but has not been, paid; or

    (c) tax on it has been remitted subject to a condition and the condition has not been complied with.

Evidence by certificate

24.—(1) A certificate of the Commissioners—

    (a) that a person was or was not, at any date, registered under this Schedule; or

    (b) that any return required by or under this Schedule has not been made or had not been made at any date; or

    (c) that any tax shown as due in any return or assessment made in pursuance of this Schedule has not been paid;

shall be sufficient evidence of the fact until the contrary is proved; and any document purporting to be such a certificate shall be deemed to be such a certificate until the contrary is proved.

(2) A photograph of any document furnished to the Commissioners for the purposes of this Schedule and certified by them to be such a photograph shall be admissible in any proceedings, whether civil or criminal, to the same extent as the document itself.

(3) Any document purporting to be a certificate under sub-paragraph (2) of this paragraph shall be deemed to be such a certificate until the contrary is proved.

Service of notices

25. A notice to be served on any person for any of the purposes of this Schedule may be served by sending it by post in a letter addressed to that person at his last or usual residence or place of business.

SCH. 7

Regulations

26.—(1) The Commissioners may by regulations made by statutory instrument make provision for any matter for which it appears to them necessary to make provision for the purpose of enabling them to discharge their functions in relation to the tax, and in particular, but without prejudice to the generality of this provision—

    (a) for requiring persons registered under this Schedule to account

for the tax payable by them by reference to such periods as
may be prescribed by the regulations and to pay the tax due
in respect of any such period within such time from the end
of the period as may be so prescribed;

(b) for the particulars to be contained in any notification under
paragraph 15 of this Schedule;

(c) for requiring persons registered under this Schedule to furnish
to persons acquiring chargeable vehicles from them certificates
in such form as may be prescribed by the regulations that the
tax on the vehicles has been or will be paid;

(d) for requiring persons not registered under this Schedule to
furnish to persons acquiring chargeable vehicles from them
statements in such form as may be prescribed by the regulations that the vehicles are chargeable vehicles on which tax
will be payable;

(e) for treating, for a limited time, as registered under this
Schedule persons who carry on the business of persons so
registered who have died or have become incapacitated;

(f) for the issue by the Commissioners of certificates stating that
the tax on any chargeable vehicle has been paid or remitted;

(g) for specifying the circumstances in which a chargeable vehicle
supplied by a person under an agreement for sale or return
is to be treated for the purposes of the tax as ceasing to be
his property in accordance with the agreement;

(h) for any other matter for which, under this Schedule, provision
may be made by regulations.

(2) Without prejudice to the generality of the preceding sub-
paragraph, the regulations may make special provision with respect
to certificates and other documents to be issued for the purposes of
the tax before the end of March 1973.

(3) A statutory instrument made under this paragraph shall be
subject to annulment in pursuance of a resolution of the Commons
House of Parliament.

Restriction on registration of chargeable vehicles

1971 c. 10.   27. Regulations made under section 23 of the Vehicles (Excise) Act
1971 may enable the Secretary of State to refuse to register a vehicle
unless he is satisfied, by such evidence as may be prescribed by the
regulations either—

(a) that the vehicle is not a chargeable vehicle; or

(b) that the tax chargeable on it has been or will be paid; or

(c) that tax on it has been remitted.

Isle of Man   Sch. 7

28.—(1) If an Act of Tynwald makes provision similar to the
provision made with respect to the car tax by this Act, Her Majesty
may by Order in Council make provision for securing that—

(a) tax is charged under either Act as if references therein to the
United Kingdom or to the Isle of Man included both the
United Kingdom and the Isle of Man, but is not charged
under both Acts on the same vehicle;

(b) persons who are registered under either this Schedule or that
Act are treated as registered also under the other; and

(c) the removal of a vehicle from the United Kingdom into the
Isle of Man or from the Isle of Man into the United Kingdom
is not treated for the purposes of either Act as an importation
or exportation of the vehicle;

and for making such modifications in those Acts and regulations made thereunder as may be requisite for those purposes; and similarly with respect to any Act passed after this Act and relating to the car tax.

(2) An Order in Council under this paragraph may include provision 1958 c. 11. for section 2 of the Isle of Man Act 1958 (Isle of Man share of certain duties) to apply as if the car tax and the tax for which provision is made by Act of Tynwald were included among the duties mentioned in subsection (4) of that section.

(3) An Order in Council under this paragraph may be varied or revoked by a subsequent Order in Council.

Appendices 3,4 and 5
The European Economic Community

COUNCIL DIRECTIVES

Appendix 3

The European Economic Community

FIRST COUNCIL DIRECTIVE
of 11 April 1967
on the harmonisation of legislation of Member States concerning turnover taxes
(67/227/EEC)

THE COUNCIL OF THE EUROPEAN ECONOMIC COMMUNITY,

HAVING REGARD to the Treaty establishing the European Economic Community, and in particular Articles 99 and 100 thereof.

HAVING REGARD to the proposal from the Commission;

HAVING REGARD to the Opinion of the European Parliament;

HAVING REGARD to the Opinion of the Economic and Social Committee;

WHEREAS the main objective of the Treaty is to establish, within the framework of an economic union, a common market within which there is healthy competition and whose characteristics are similar to those of a domestic market;

WHEREAS the attainment of this objective presupposes the prior application in Member States of legislation concerning turnover taxes such as will not distort conditions of competition or hinder the free movement of goods and services within the common market;

WHEREAS the legislation at present in force does not meet these requirements; whereas it is therefore in the interest of the common market to achieve such harmonisation of legislation concerning turnover taxes as will eliminate as far as possible, factors which may distort conditions of competition, whether at national or Community level, and make it possible subsequently to achieve the aim of abolishing the imposition of tax on importation and the remission of tax on exportation in trade between Member States;

WHEREAS, in the light of the studies made, it has become clear that such harmonisation must result in the abolition of cumulative multi-stage taxes and in the adoption by all Member States of a common system of value added tax;

WHEREAS a system of value added tax achieves the highest degree of simplicity and of neutrality when the tax is levied in as general a manner as possible and when its scope covers all stages of production and distribution and the provision of services; whereas it is therefore in the interest of the common market and of Member States to adopt a common system which shall also apply to the retail trade;

WHEREAS, however, the application of that tax to retail trade might in some Member States meet with practical and political difficulties; whereas, therefore, Member States should be permitted, subject to prior consultation to apply the common system only up to and including the wholesale trade stage, and to apply, as appropriate, a separate complementary tax at the retail trade stage, or at the preceding stage;

WHEREAS it is necessary to proceed by stages, since the harmonisation of turnover taxes will lead in Member States to substantial alterations in tax structure and will have appreciable consequences in the budgetary, economic and social fields;

WHEREAS the replacement of the cumulative multi-stage tax systems in force in the majority of Member States by the common system of value added tax is bound, even if the rates and exemption are not harmonised at the same time, to result in neutrality in competition, in that within each country similar goods bear the same tax burden, whatever the length of the production and distribution chain, and that in international trade the amount of the tax burden borne by goods is known so that an exact equalisation of that amount may be ensured; whereas, therefore, provision should be made, in the first stage for adoption by all Member States of the common system of value added tax, without an accompanying harmonisation of rates and exemptions;

WHEREAS it is not possible to foresee at present how and within what period the harmonisation of turnover taxes can achieve the aim of abolishing the imposition of tax on importation and the remission of tax on exportation in trade between Member States; whereas it is therefore preferable that the second stage and the measures to be taken in respect of that stage should be determined later on the basis of proposals made by the Commission to the Council;

HAS ADOPTED THIS DIRECTIVE:

Article 1
Member States shall replace their present system of turnover taxes by the common system of value added tax defined in Article 2.

In each Member State the legislation to effect this replacement shall be enacted as rapidly as possible, so that it can enter into force on a date to be fixed by the Member State in the light of the conjunctural situation; this date shall not be later than 1 January 1970.

From the entry into force of such legislation, the Member State shall not maintain or introduce any measure providing for flat rate equalisation of turnover taxes on importation or exportation in trade between Member States.

Article 2
The principle of the common system of value added tax involves the application to goods and services of a general tax on consumption exactly proportional to the price of the goods and services, whatever the number of transactions which take place in the production and distribution process before the stage at which tax is charged.

On each transaction, value added tax, calculated on the price of the goods or services at the rate applicable to such goods or services, shall be chargeable after deduction of the amount of value added tax borne directly by the various cost components.

The common system of value added tax shall be applied up to and including the retail trade stage.

However, until the abolition of the imposition of tax on importation and the remission of tax on exportation in trade between Member States, Member States may, subject to the consultation provided for in Article 5, apply this system only up to and including the wholesale trade stage, and may apply, as appropriate, a separate complementary tax at the retail trade stage or at the preceding stage..

Article 3
The Council shall issue, on a proposal from the Commission a second Directive concerning the structure of, and the procedure for applying, the common system of value added tax.

Article 4
In order to enable the Council to discuss this and if possible to take decisions before the end of the transitional period, the Commission shall submit to the Council, before the end of 1968, proposals as to how and within what period the harmonisation of turnover taxes can achieve the aim of abolishing the imposition of tax on importation and the remission of tax on exportation in trade between Member States, while ensuring the neutrality of those taxes as regards the origin of the goods or services.

In this connection, particular account shall be taken of the relationship between direct and indirect taxes, which differs in the various Member States; of the effects of an alteration in tax systems on the tax and budget policy of Member States; and of the influence which tax systems have on conditions of competition and on social conditions in the Community

Article 5
Should a Member State intend to exercise the power provided for in the last paragraph of Article 2, it shall so inform the Commission in good time having regard to Article 102 of the Treaty.

Article 6
This Directive is addressed to the Member States.
Done at Brussels, 11 April 1967.
For the Council
The President
R VAN ELSANDE

The United Kingdom will have six months after the date of accession within which to bring this Directive into force.

Appendix 4

The European Economic Community

SECOND COUNCIL DIRECTIVE

of 11 April 1967

on the harmonisation of legislation of Member States concerning turnover taxes — Structure and procedures for application of the common system of value added tax —

(67/228/EEC)

THE COUNCIL OF THE EUROPEAN COMMUNITY,

HAVING REGARD to the Treaty establishing the European Economic Community, and in particular Articles 99 and 100 thereof;

HAVING REGARD to the First Council Directive of 11 April 1967 (1) on the harmonisation of legislation of Member States concerning turnover taxes;

HAVING REGARD to the proposal from the Commission;

HAVING REGARD to the Opinion of the European Parliament;

HAVING REGARD to the Opinion of the Economic and Social Committee;

WHEREAS the relacement of the turnover taxes in force in Member States by a common system of value added tax is intended as a means of attaining the objective set out in the First Directive;

WHEREAS, until the abolition of the imposition of tax on importation and the remission of tax on exportation, it is possible to grant Member States substantial autonomy in determining the rate or differential rates of tax;

WHEREAS it is also possible to accept on a transitional basis certain differences in the procedure for applying the tax in Member States; whereas it is, however, necessary to make provision for appropriate procedures to ensure neutrality in competition between Member States and to restrict progressively or to abolish the differences in question, so that national systems of value added tax may be brought into alignment, therby preparing the way for the attainment of the objective set out in Article 4 of the First Directive;

WHEREAS, in order to enable the system to be applied in a simple and neutral manner, and to keep the standard rate of tax within reasonable limits it is necessary to limit special systems and exceptional measures;

WHEREAS the system of value added tax makes it possible, where appropriate, for social and economic reasons, to effect reductions or increases in the tax burden on certain goods and services by means of a differentiation in the rates, but the introduction of zero rates gives rise to difficulties, so that it is highly desirable to limit strictly the number of exemptions and to make the deductions considered necessary by applying reduced rates which are high enough to permit in normal circumstances the deduction of the tax paid at the preceding stage, which moreover achieves in general the same result as that at present obtained by the application of exemptions in cumulative multi-stage systems;

WHEREAS it has proved possible to leave Member States themselves to make rules concerning the numerous services whose cost has no influence on the prices of goods, and the systems to be applied in the case of small undertakings, subject, as regards the latter, to prior consultation;

WHEREAS it has proved necessary to provide for special systems for the application of the value added tax to the agricultural sector and to request the Commission to submit to the Council, as soon as possible proposals to this effect;

WHEREAS it is necessary to provide for a rather large number of special provisions covering interpretation, derogations and certain detailed application procedures, and to establish a list of the services compulsorily subject to the common system; and whereas these provisions and this list should appear in the Annexes forming an integrál part of this Directive;

HAS ADOPTED THIS DIRECTIVE:

Article 1

Member States shall introduce, in accordance with a common system a tax on turnover (hereinafter called "value added tax").

The structure of, and procedures for applying, this tax shall be established by Member States in accordance with the provision of the following Articles and of Annexes A and B.

Article 2

The following shall be subject to the value added tax:
(a) The supply of goods and the provision of services within the territory of the country by a taxable person against payment;
(b) the importation of goods.

Article 3

"Territory of the country" means the territory in which the State concerned applies the value added tax; this territory shall, as a general rule, include the whole of the national territory, including territorial waters.

Article 4

"Taxable person" means any person who independently and habitually engages in transactions pertaining to the activities of producers, traders or persons providing services, whether or not for gain.

Article 5

1 "Supply of goods" means the transfer of the right to dispose of tangible property as owner.
2 The following shall also be considered as supply within the meaning of paragraph 1:
(a) the actual handing over of goods, under a contract which provides for the hiring of goods for a certain period, or the sale on deferred terms of goods in both cases subject to a clause to the effect that ownership shall pass at the latest upon payment of the final instalment due;
(b) the transfer, by order of a public authority, of ownership in goods against payment of compensation;
(c) the transfer of goods pursuant to a contract under which commission is payable on purchase or sale;
(d) the delivery of movable property produced under a contract for work, that is

to say the handing over by a contractor to his customer of movable property which he has made from materials and objects entrusted to him by the customer for this purpose, whether or not the contractor has provided a part of the products used;

(e) the delivery up of works of construction, including those in which movable property is incorporated in immovable property.

3   The following shall be treated as supply against payment:

(a) the appropriation by a taxable person, from his undertaking, of goods which he applies to his own private use or transfers free of charge;

(b) the use for the needs of his undertaking, by a taxable person, of goods produced or extracted by him or by another person on his behalf.

4   The place of supply shall be deemed as being

(a) in cases where the goods are dispatched or transported either by the supplier or by the consignee, or by a third person: the place where the goods were at the time when the dispatch or transport to the consignee began;

(b) in cases where the goods are not dispatched or transported: the place where the goods were at the time of supply.

5   The chargeable event shall occur at the moment when delivery is effected. In the case, however, of supply involving payments on account before delivery, it may be provided that the chargeable event shall already have occurred at the moment of issue of the invoice or, at the latest, at the moment of receipt of the payment, in respect of the whole of the amount invoiced or received.

Article 6

1   "Provision of services" means any transaction which does not constitute a supply of goods within the meaning of Article 5.

2   The rules laid down in this Directive as regards the taxation of the provision of services shall be compulsorily applicable only to services listed in Annex B.

3   The place of the provision of services shall, as a general rule, be regarded as being the place where the services provided, the right transferred or granted, or the object hired, is used or enjoyed.

4   The chargeable event shall occur at the moment when the service is provided. In the case, however, of the provision of service of indeterminate length or exceeding a certain period or involving payments on account, it may be provided that the chargeable event shall already have occurred at the moment of issue of the invoice or, at the latest, at the moment of the receipt of the payment on account, in respect of the whole of the amount invoiced or received.

Article 7

1   "Importation of goods" means the entry of such goods into the "territory of the country" within the meaning of Article 3.

2   At importation, the chargeable event shall occur at the time of such entry. Member States may, however, link the chargeable event and the date when payment of customs duties or other import taxes, charges and levies falls due.

The same link may be established, as regards the chargeable event and the date when payment of value added tax falls due, in respect of the supply of imported goods placed under a system of suspension of customs duties or other taxes charges or levies.

Article 8

The basis of assessment shall be:

(a) in the case of supply of goods and of the provision of services, everything which makes up the consideration for the supply of the goods or the provision of services, including all expenses and taxes except the value added tax itself;

(b) in the case of the transactions referred to in Article 5(3)(a) and (b), the purchase price of the goods or of like goods or, if there is no purchase price, the cost price;

(c) in the case of importation of goods, the customs value, plus all duties, taxes charges and levies due by reason of importation, except the value added tax itself. The same basis of assessment shall apply when the goods are exempt from customs duties or are not subject to *ad valorem* customs duties.

In the case of importation of goods, each Member State may add to the basis of assessment the incidental expenses (packing, transport, insurance, etc) arising up to the place of destination which have not been included in that basis.

Article 9

1 The standard rate of value added tax shall be fixed by each Member State at a percentage of the basis of assessment which shall be the same for the supply of goods and for the provision of services.

2 In certain cases, the supply of goods and the provision of services may, however, be subject to increased rates or to reduced rates. Each reduced rate shall be determined in such a manner that the amount of value added tax resulting from the application of this rate shall normally permit the deduction of the whole of the value added tax which is deductable under Article 11.

3 The rate applicable to importation of goods shall be that which is applied in the territory of the country to the supply of like goods.

Article 10

1 The following shall be exempted from value added tax on conditions laid down by each Member State:

(a) the supply of goods consigned or transported to places outside the territory in which the State concerned applies value added tax;

(b) the provision of services relating to goods covered by (a) or in transit.

2 The provision of services relating to importations of goods may, subject to the consultations mentioned in Article 16, be exempted from value added tax.

3 Each Member State may, subject to the consultations mentioned in Article 16, determine the other exemptions which it considers necessary.

Article 11

1 Where goods and services are used for the purposes of his undertaking, the taxable person shall be authorised to deduct from the tax for which he is liable:

(a) the value added tax invoiced to him in respect of goods supplied to him or in respect of services rendered to him;

(b) the value added tax paid in respect of imported goods;

(c) the value added tax which he has paid in respect of the use of goods referred to in Article 5(3)(b).

2 Value added tax on goods and services used in non-taxable or exempt transactions shall not be deductible.

The taxable person shall however be authorised to make the deduction if the supply of goods or the provision of services takes place abroad or is exempt under Article 10(1) or (2).

As regards goods and services which are used both in transactions giving entitlement to deduction and in transactions which do not give entitlement to deduction, deduction shall only be allowed for that part of the value added tax which is proportional to the amount relating to the transactions giving entitlement to deduction (*pro rata* rule).

3 The deduction shall be made from the value added tax due for the period during which the deductible tax is invoiced in the case of paragraph I(a) or paid in the case of paragraph I(b) and (c) immediate deductions).

In the case of a partial deduction under paragraph 2 the amount of the deduction shall be provisionally determined in accordance with criteria established by each Member State and finally adjusted after the end of the year when the *pro rata* figure for the year of acquisition has been calculated.

As regards capital goods, the adjustment shall be effected on the basis of the variations of the *pro rata* figure which have occurred during a period of five years including the year during which the goods were acquired; the adjustment shall apply each year to only one fifth of the tax borne by capital goods.

4 Certain goods and services may be excluded from the deduction system, in particular those capable of being exclusively or partially used for the private needs of the taxable person or of his staff.

Article 12

1 Every taxable person shall keep sufficiently detailed accounts to permit application of the value added tax and inspection by the tax authorities.

2 Every taxable person shall issue an invoice in respect of goods supplied and services provided by him to another taxable person.

3 Every taxable person shall each month lodge a declaration showing, in respect of transactions carried out during the preceding month, all the information required to calculate the tax and the deductions to be made. Every taxable person shall pay the amount of the value added tax when lodging the declaration.

Article 13

Should a Member State consider that, in exceptional cases, special measures should be adopted in order to prevent certain frauds, it shall so inform the Commission and the other Member States.

Should there, within one month, be objections from one or more States or from the Commission, the request for derogation shall be brought before the Council, which shall act on a proposal from the Commission within three months.

Should it appear from the conclusion of the Commission that only a simplification of the charging procedure or a measure designed to prevent fraud is involved, the Council shall act by a qualified majority on the derogation request.

Should it appear, on the contrary, from those conclusions that the proposed measure might be prejudicial to the very principles of the system introduced by this Directive, and in particular to neutrality in competition between Member States, the Council shall act unanimously.

In either case, the Council shall act in accordance with the same procedure as regards the period of application of such measures.

The State concerned may not apply the proposed measures until the period for entering objections has expired or, where there have been objections, until after the Council's decision, if such decision is favourable.

The provisions shall cease to be applicable when the imposition of tax on importation and the remission of tax on exportation are abolished in trade between Member States.

Article 14

Each Member State may, subject to the consultations mentioned in Article 16, apply to small undertakings whose subjection to the normal system of value added tax would meet with difficulties the special system best suited to national requirements and possibilities.

Article 15

1 The Commission shall submit to the Council, as soon as possible, proposals for Directives on common procedures for applying value added tax to transactions relating to agricultural products.

2 Until the date fixed in the Directives referred to in paragraph 1 for the application of such common procedures, each Member State may, subject to the consultations mentioned in Article 16, apply to undertakings in the agricultural sector whose subjection to the normal system of value added tax would meet with difficulties the special system best suited to national requirements and possibilities.

Article 16

Where a Member State must, in accordance with the provisions of this Directive, enter into consultations, it shall refer to the matter to the Commission in good time, having regard to the application of Article 102 of the Treaty.

Article 17

With a view to the transition from the present system of turnover taxes to the common system of value added tax, Member States may:

   adopt transitional measures to levy the tax in advance;

   apply, during a certain transitional period, in respect of capital goods the method of deduction by annual instalments (deductions *pro rata temporis*);

   exclude, in whole or in part, during a certain transitional period, capital goods from the deduction system provided for in Article 11;

and, subject to the consultations mentioned in Article 16:

   authorise (in order to grant relief, total or partial, but general in scope, from the turnover tax charged up to the time of introducing value added tax) standard deductions in respect of capital goods not yet written off and of stocks in hand at that time. Member States may, however, restrict such deductions to goods exported during a period of one year from the introduction of value added tax. In that event, such deductions shall only be allowed in respect of stocks in hand at the time referred to above and exported in an unaltered state;

   provide for reduced rates or even exemptions with refund, if appropriate, of the tax paid at the preceding stage, where the total incidence of such measures does not exceed that of the reliefs applied under the present system. Such measures may only be taken for clearly defined social reasons and for the benefit of the final consumer, and may not remain in force after the abolition of the imposition of tax on importation and the remission of tax on exportation in trade between Member States.

Article 18

The Commission shall, after consulting the Member States, submit to the Council for the first time on 1 January 1972 and every two years thereafter a report on the operation of the common system of value added tax in Member States.

Article 19

The Council shall, in the interest of the common market, adopt at the proper time, on a proposal from the Commission, the appropriate Directives to complete the common system of value added tax and in particular to restrict progressively or to abolish measures adopted by Member States in derogation from this system, so that national systems of value added tax may be brought into alignment thereby preparing the way for the attainment of the objective set out in Article 4 of the First Directive.

Article 20
The Annexes shall form an integral part of this Directive.

Article 21
This Directive is addressed to the Member States.
Done at Brussels, 11 April 1967.
For the Council
The President
R VAN ELSLANDE

ANNEXE A

1 Regarding Article 3
If A Member State intends to apply value added tax in a territory smaller than its national territory, it shall enter into the consultations mentioned in Article 16.

2 Regarding Article 4
The expression "activities of producers, traders, or persons providing services" is to be understood in a wide sense and to cover all economic activities, including, therefore, activities of the extractive industries, agriculture and the professions.

If a Member State intends not to tax certain activities, it should achieve its purpose by means of exemptions rather than by excluding from the scope of the tax persons pursuing such activities.

Member States may also consider as a "taxable person" anyone who engages occasionally in the transactions referred to in Article 4.

The expression "independently" is intended in particular to exclude from taxation wage-earners who are bound to their employer by a contract of service. This expression also makes it possible for each Member State not to consider as separate taxable persons, but as one single taxable person, persons who, although independent from the legal point of view, are, however, organically linked to one another by economic, financial or organisational relationships Any Member State intending to adopt such a system enter into the consultations mentioned in Article 16.

States, regional and local government bodes and other public corporate bodies shall not as a rule be considered as taxable persons in respect of activities which they pursue in their official capacity as official authorities.

If, however, they pursue activities as producers traders, or providers of services, they may be considered as liable to tax in respect of such activities.

3 Regarding Article 5(1)
"Tangible property" means both movable and immovable tangible property.

The supply of electric current, gas, heat, refrigeration and the like shall be considered as supply of goods.

In the case of contribution to a company of the whole or part of the contributor's assets. Member States may regard the benefiting company as the successor in title of the contributor.

4 Regarding Article 5(2)(a)
For the purposes of this Directive, the contract referred to in Article 5(2)(a) must not be subdivided into part hire and part sale, but shall be regarded, as soon as concluded, as a contract involving a taxable supply.

5 Regarding Article 5(2)(d) and (e)

Member States which, for specifically national reason, cannot consider the transactions referred to in Article 5(2)(d) and (e) as supply shall classify them in the category of provision of services, subjecting them to the rate which would be applicable to them if they were considered as supply.

The following, shall be considered as "works of construction":

the construction of buildings, bridges, roads, ports, etc, in performance of a building contract;

earth-moving and planting of gardens;

installation work (of central heating, for example);

repairs to buildings, other than current maintenance.

6 Regarding Article 5(3)(a)

As regards the appropriation of goods in an unaltered state bought by a taxable person, Member States may, instead of taxing, forbid deduction or adjust it if deduction has already been affected. However, appropriation for giving gifts of small value and samples, which from the tax point of view may be classified as overhead expenses, shall not be considered as taxable supply. Moreover, the provisions of Article 11(2) shall not be applicable to such appropriations.

7 Regarding Article 5(3)(b)

This provision shall only be applied to ensure equality of taxation between on the one hand, goods purchased and intended for the needs of the undertaking, and in respect of which there is no entitlement to immediate or complete deduction, and, on the other hand, goods produced or extracted by the taxable person or on his behalf by a third person which are also used for the same needs. 8

8 Regarding Article 5(3)(a)

The "chargeable event" means the event giving rise to the tax.

9 Regarding Article 6(1)

The definition of provision of services given in this paragraph involves classification of, inter alia, the following as provision of services:

the assignment of intangible property;

the carrying out of an obligation to refrain from doing something;

the carrying out of a service rendered by order of a public authority;

the carrying out of work on goods, if such work is not considered as supply within the meaning of Article 5(2)(d) and (e) as, for example, current maintenance work, the laundering of linen, etc.

This definition shall not prevent taxation by Member States of certain transactions engaged in by a taxable person as services "rendered to oneself" when such a measure proves necessary in order to avoid distortion of competition.

10 Regarding Article 6(2)

Member States shall refrain, as far as possible, from granting exemption from tax in respect of the provision of the services listed in Annexe B.

11 Regarding Article 6(3)

The Council shall, acting unanimously on a proposal from the Commission, lay down, before 1 January 1970, special rules concerning certain services for which such rules may prove necessary, derogating where appropriate from the provisions of Article 6(3). Until those rules have been laid down, each Member State may, in order to simplify the procedure for charging the tax, derogate from the provisions of Article 6(3); it shall, however, take the necessary steps to avoid double taxation or non-taxation.

12 *Regarding Article 8*
Any Member State which applies value added tax only up to and including the wholesale stage may, in the case of goods sold by retai l by a taxable person, reduce the basis of assessment by a certain percentage; the basis thus reduced shall not, however, be lower than the purchase or cost price plus where appropriate, the amount of the customs duties (including levies), taxes and charges on the goods (except value added tax), even if payment thereof has been suspended.

In the case of importation of goods sold by retail, the same reduction shall be applied to the basis assessment.

It shall be left to Member States to define, in accordance with their national concepts, the concept of "sale of goods by retail".

Each Member State may, subject to the consu tations mentioned in Article 16, lay down, as a measure to prevent fraud and in respect of specified goods and services, that, in derogation from Article 8, the basis of assessment shall not be lower than a minimum basis determined by its national law.

13 *Regarding Article 8(a)*
The expression "consideration" means everything received in return for the supply of goods or the provision of services, including incidental expenses (packing, transport, insurance, etc.) that is to say not only the cash amount charged, but also, for example, the value of the goods received in exchange or, in the case of goods or services supplied by order of a public authority, the amount of the compensation received.

This provisions shall not, however, prevent each Member State which considers it necessary for the achievement of greater neutrality in competition from being able to exclude from the basis of assessment in respect of supply the incidental expenses arising as from the place of supply as defined in Article 5(4) and to tax such expenses as consideration for the provision of services.

Further, the expenses paid in the same and for the account of the customer which are shown in the accounts of the supply as transitory items shall not be included in the basis of assessment.

The customs duties and other charges, taxes etc, paid at importation by agents and other intermediaries in customs clearance including forwarding agents. under their own name, may also be exluded from the basis of assessment corresponding to the services they have provided.

14 *Regarding Article 8(c)*
In intra-Community trade, Member States shall endeavour to apply to importations of goods and basis of assessment which corresponds, as far as possible to that used for supply made within the territory of the country; this basis shall include the same components as those taken into account pursuant to Article 8(c).

Until the abolition of the imposition of tax on importation and the remission of tax on exportation in trade between Member States at the latest, and subject to the consultations mentioned in Article 16, each Member State may apply to importations of goods from third countries a basis of assessment which corresponds, as far as possible, to that used for supply within the territory of the country; this basis shall include the same components as those taken into account pursuant to Article 8(c).

15 *Regarding Article 9(2)*
Where this paragraph is applied to the transport services referred to in Annex B, item 5, it must be so applied as to ensure equality of treatment as between the different modes of transport.

16 *Regarding Article 10(1)(a)*
Relief from tax as provided for in this provision refers to the supply of goods directly exported, that is to say supply made by the exporter. Member States may, however, extend exemption to supply made at the preceding stage.

17 *Regarding Article 10(1)(b)*
Member States may, however, refrain from granting this exemption if relief from the value added tax charged on the provision of these services is effected in favour of the beneficiary of the services by means of deductions. Moreover, Member States may, except in the case of the provision of services relating to goods in transit, restrict such exemption of the provision of services relating to goods the supply of which inside the country is taxable.

18 *Regarding Article 19(2)*
This provision relates in particular to the provision of international transport services at importation and to port services.

19 *Regarding Article 10(2) and (3)*
Where these paragraphs are applied to the transport services referred to in Annex B, item 5, they must be so applied as to ensure equality of treatment as between the different modes of transport.

20 *Regarding Article 11(1)(a)*
In the case provided for in Article 55(5), second sentence, and Article 6(4), second sentence, the deduction may be made as soon as the invoice is received, even though the goods have not yet been supplied or the services rendered.

21 *Regarding Article 11(2), second subparagraph*
Member States may, however, restrict the right to deduction to transactions relating to goods the suuply of which inside the country is taxable.

22 *Regarding Article 11(2), third subparagraph*
The *pro rata* figure shall, in general, be determined in respect of all the transactions carried out by the taxable person (general *pro rata* figure). However a taxable person may, exceptionally, obtain administrative permission to determine special *pro rata* figures for certain sectors of his activities..

23 *Regarding Article 11(3), first subparagraph*
Subject to the consultations mentioned in Article 16, each Member State may, on conjunctural grounds, partially or wholly exclude capital goods from the deduction system, or apply in respect of such goods, instead of the method of immediate deductions, that of annual instalments (deductions *pro rata temporis*).

24 *Regarding Article 11(3), third subparagraph*
Member States may specify certain tolerances in order to limit the number of adjustments in the event of variations in the annual *pro rata* figure as compared with the initial *pro rata* figure which serviced as a basis for deductions in the case of capital goods.

25 *Regarding Article 12(2)*

The invoice must show separately the price exclusive of tax and the corresponding tax for each different rate, together with any exemption.

Each Member State may, in special cases, provide for derogations from this rule and also from the obligation laid down in Article 12(2). Such derogations, however, must be strictly limited.

Notwithstanding the other measures to be taken by Member States to ensure payment of the tax and to prevent fraud, all persons, whether taxable or not, who show the value added tax on an invoice, must pay the amount thereof.

26 *Regarding Article 12(1)*

Each Member State may, for practical reasons, shorten the period laid down in Article 12(3) or authorise certain taxable persons to lodge the declaration quarterly, half-yearly or annually.

During the first six months of each year the taxable person shall, where appropriate, lodge a declaration concerning all the previous year's transactions, and including all the particulars necessary for any adjustments.

Each Member State shall, as regards importation of goods adopt measures governing the procedure in respect of the declaration and of the payment which must ensue.

27 *Regarding Article 14*

Where this Article is applied to the transport services referred to in Annex B, item 5, it must be so applied as to ensure equality of treatment as between the different modes of transport.

28 *Regarding Article 17, fourth indent*

Stocks may be valued inter alia by reference to the transactions carried out during preceding years by the taxable persons.

ANNEXE B

List of the services referred to in Article 6(2):

1 assignment of patents, trade marks and other similar rights, and the granting of licences in respect of such rights;
2 work, other than that referred to in Article 5(2)(d) on tangible movable property, carried out for a taxable person;
3 provision of services to prepare or coordinate the carrying out of works of construction, as, for example, services provided by architects and by firms providing on-site supervision of works;
4 commercial advertising services;
5 transport and storage of goods, and ancillary services;
6 hiring of tangible movable property to a taxable person;
7 provision of staff to a taxable person;
8 services provided by consultants, engineers, planning offices and similar services, in scientific, economic or technical fields;
9 the carrying out of an obligation to refrain from exercising, in whole or in part, a business activity or a right included in this list;
10 the services of forwarding agents, brokers, business agents and other independent intermediaries, in so far as they relate to supply of importation of goods or the provision of services included in th s list.

The United Kingdom will have six months after the date of accession within which to bring this Directive into force.

Appendix 5

The European Economic Communities

THIRD COUNCIL DIRECTIVE
of 9 December 1969
on the harmonisation of legislation of Member States concerning turnover taxes
introduction of value added tax in Member States
(69/463/EEC)

THE COUNCIL OF THE EUROPEAN COMMUNITIES,

HAVING REGARD to the Treaty establishing the European Economic Community, and in particular Acticles 99 and 100 thereof;

HAVING REGARD to the proposal from the Commission;

HAVING REGARD to the Opinion of the European Parliament ([1]);

HAVING REGARD to the Opinion of the Economic and Social Committee ([2]);

WHEREAS the Italian Republic and the Kingdom of Belgium made known to the Commission, on 14th July and 12 September 1969 respectively, that they were not in a position to meet the final date of 1 January 1970 for the introduction of value added tax as provided in Article 1 of the First Council Directive of 11 April 1967 ([3]) on the harmonisation of legislation of Member States concerning turnover taxes; whereas, consequently, those Member States have asked for a further period of two years and one year respectively for the introduction of that tax;

WHEREAS the Kingdom of Belgium considers that it is not in a position to apply value added tax on the date laid down, mainly for conjunctural and budgetary reasons peculiar to Belgium;

WHEREAS the Italian Republic has pointed out that a proposal for the general reform of taxes has now been tabled for consideration and adoption by Parliament, which has not yet considered this problem; whereas, according to that proposal, the appropriate legislation must be adopted before 31 October 1970; whereas, consequently, that Member State is not in a position to apply value added tax on the date laid down;

WHEREAS an additional period may be granted only if it is kept to a minimum;

WHEREAS, in these circumstances, introduction of value added tax may not be delayed beyond 1 January 1972;

WHEREAS one of the main objectives of the First Directive mentioned above is, through the introduction of value added tax on 1 January 1970, to establish conditions making it possible to avoid competition being distorted by turnover taxes;

WHEREAS that objective cannot be attained by 1 January 1970, in particular as regards trade, since these Member States will continue to apply, by means of turnover taxes, average rates of equalisation of the internal tax burden;

WHEREAS Member States which are not in a position to introduce value added tax by 1 January 1970 should not increase their average equalisation rates in operation on 1 October 1969;

HAS ADOPTED THIS DIRECTIVE:

Article 1
The date of 1 January 1972 shall be substituted for that of 1 January 1970 laid down in Article 1 of the First Directive of 11 April 1967.

Article 2
For the purpose of this Directive, "average rates" means the rates of counter-vailing charges on importation and of repayments on exportation introduced so as to equalise, as regards national products, the burden resulting from the cumulative multi-stage turnover tax at the various stages of production, excluding the tax on sales by the final producer.

Article 3
The average rates in force on 1 October 1969 may not be increased.

However, the average rates in operation on that date shall be adapted to any later changes in the rates of turnover tax.

Article 4
This Directive is addressed to the Member States.
Done at Brussels, 9 December 1969.
For the Council
The President
H J DE KOSTER

The United Kingdom will have six months after the date of accession within which to bring this Directive into force.

Index